Is Your Child Psychic?

Is Your Child Psychic?

A Guide to Developing Your Child's Innate Abilities

DR. ALEX TANOUS *and*

KATHERINE FAIR DONNELLY

JEREMY P. TARCHER/PENGUIN

a member of Penguin Group (USA) Inc.

New York

JEREMY P. TARCHER/PENGUIN
Published by the Penguin Group
Penguin Group (USA) Inc., 375 Hudson Street, New York, New York 10014, USA •
Penguin Group (Canada), 90 Eglinton Avenue East, Suite 700, Toronto,
Ontario M4P 2Y3, Canada (a division of Pearson Penguin Canada Inc.) •
Penguin Books Ltd, 80 Strand, London WC2R 0RL, England • Penguin Ireland,
25 St Stephen's Green, Dublin 2, Ireland (a division of Penguin Books Ltd) •
Penguin Group (Australia), 250 Camberwell Road, Camberwell, Victoria 3124, Australia
(a division of Pearson Australia Group Pty Ltd) • Penguin Books India Pvt Ltd,
11 Community Centre, Panchsheel Park, New Delhi–110 017, India •
Penguin Group (NZ), 67 Apollo Drive, Rosedale, North Shore 0632,
New Zealand (a division of Pearson New Zealand Ltd) •
Penguin Books (South Africa) (Pty) Ltd, 24 Sturdee Avenue,
Rosebank, Johannesburg 2196, South Africa

Penguin Books Ltd, Registered Offices: 80 Strand, London WC2R 0RL, England

Most Tarcher/Penguin books are available at special quantity discounts for bulk purchase
for sales promotions, premiums, fund-raising, and educational needs. Special books or
book excerpts also can be created to fit specific needs. For details, write
Penguin Group (USA) Inc. Special Markets, 375 Hudson Street, New York, NY 10014.

Library of Congress Cataloging-in-Publication Data

Tanous, Alex, date.
Is your child psychic? : a guide to developing your child's innate abilities /
Alex Tanous & Katherine Fair Donnelly. —1st Jeremy P. Tarcher ed.
p.   cm.
Includes bibliographical references and index.
ISBN 978-1-58542-738-3
1. Exceptional children.   2. Children—Psychic ability.   3. Psychic games.
I. Donnelly, Katherine Fair.   II. Title.
HQ 773.T36   2009   2009024355
133.8083—dc22

Printed in the United States of America
1   3   5   7   9   10   8   6   4   2

BOOK DESIGN BY NICOLE LAROCHE

To the children of the world . . .
and their parents and teachers

Contents

Part Three

Tests and Games for Developing Psychic Abilities

Introduction

Your radio is playing. The music is melodious, and you feel like humming along with it. The rhythmic energy reaches through to you even though the radio is not connected to any electrical outlet. All the vibrations are there, simply changed in the mechanism of the radio; it is transmitting sound, and you are receiving music. In a similar way, our minds have a capacity to communicate. And just as there are many stations on the radio, so are there many channels of the mind.

In this book, the authors will try to direct your attention to understanding *all* the channels of a child's mind and the various forms of communication the child is capable of utilizing. What purpose does the radio serve in our daily affairs? Not only do we listen to music, but by the mere flick of a dial we can hear news of the entire world. Another flick, and we hear a live baseball game at the very instant it is being played. Why is it, then, that we express surprise that children can convey messages by what seem to be extraordinary means but are actually as simple as hearing a baseball game on the radio?

Parents will find when listening to conversations among children that their ESP experiences are quite ordinary; that is, they are of the type that occur frequently. A child's psychic experience may at first appear extraordinary to a parent because the information the child received was obtained through channels different from those ordinarily accepted. However, had the child answered the telephone and received the same information, his or her parents would have considered it perfectly acceptable. Why, then, should it be difficult to accept that a child is relaying information received in a new or different way?

Let's turn to some of those channels of the child's mind that encompass areas such as *telepathy, clairvoyance,* and *precognition.* What do these technical-sounding words mean, and why do we call them "communication channels"? These three words are important terms for the type of experience conveyed through that particular means, or channel. They describe methods of transmission and communication and are no more to be feared than the labels given to other means of transmission and communication, such as *radio* and *television.* In the future, *telepathy, clairvoyance,* and *precognition* will probably be as commonplace. But it is the present we are concerned with, and the needs of children tuned into these channels who may be confused and anxious about their experiences because their parents and teachers don't understand the "channels." The primary purpose of this book is to serve as a guide for creative parents and teachers by helping them to understand children who are curious about their experiences and who want questions answered. The only way parents and teachers can offer answers is to know what the questions are. Some of both are offered in this primer, but work in this area is still in its infancy. It may be generations before we fully understand such children's experiences as these:

"Mommy, don't go upstairs. The telephone is going to ring. Grandma wants to talk to you." When seconds later the phone rings and Grandma is indeed on the phone, Mommy jokes about her child having ESP but thinks nothing more of the incident, even though it happens time and time again, with different callers.

"*Daddy, I had a bad dream in the night that Mr. Wilson was having an accident and his car hit a tree.*" Daddy tells the child it was just a bad dream and to go back to sleep. Days later when the parent learns that Mr. Wilson accidentally has crashed his auto into a tree, he is puzzled and concerned. How did his child know this—before it happened? And what should he as a parent do if his child has more "bad" dreams?

"*Mommy, Aunt Mary is coming to see us today.*" Because her sister Mary lives in the next town, many miles away, and always calls before coming to visit, the mother calls this wishful thinking on the part of her child. Later in the afternoon when Aunt Mary does arrive for an unexpected visit, Mommy is a little disconcerted but dismisses it as coincidence, even though it is not the first time something like this has happened. The child is "always saying crazy things."

"*Daddy, my friend wants me to go out and play with him.*" Not seeing anyone with the boy, the father tells him to stop making up stories or he will be punished.

"*Mommy, I floated through the door and then I was flying very high, but I could see me still down in my bed. Then, after a while, I decided to come back so I floated back into my room and up to the ceiling and then back to my bed.*" Mommy tells her daughter to go back to sleep and not bother her. The child asks, "Do you go flying, Mommy?" The mother rebukes the child. "No, and neither do you, Miss Smarty-pants. Now go back to bed." The child is perplexed and in the future does not tell her mother any more about the "flying." No effort has been made to understand what has taken place.

"*Let's go into the other room where the cat is. I want to play with the rocking horse in there.*" Knowing that she and her child have never visited here before, the woman is amazed to find when entering the next room that there *is* a cat and there *is* a rocking horse in the corner. The mother simply laughs off the situation as "spooky."

How can a parent deal with these experiences? Must one have special training? Just what is involved in these experiences? In this book, the authors present straightforward explanations for parents who want to gain insight into the nature of their child's experiences. As you read on, you will learn not only the specific ways in which these forms of abilities help the child but also how they help parents and teachers as well. Clairvoyance, telepathy, and precognition work in very positive ways to help a child utilize his or her natural abilities in a creative and productive manner. Various ESP (extrasensory perception) tests conducted by responsible and highly respected workers in this field have been shown to act as a barometer of the relationship between teacher and child. In the home they can provide a similar gauge in understanding the real emotions between parent and child.

A child who is going to develop in a healthy and normal way will have psychic ability that is disciplined and developed. This applies equally to parents, who suddenly may realize that they, too, have had unusual experiences they cannot explain. Perhaps they vaguely remember an experience they had many years ago, but think of it in terms of "coincidence" or have never told anyone about it for fear of ridicule. They may be embarrassed to speak of it for fear of being called "peculiar," or they may have simply dismissed the experience.

ESP is not supernatural, and it is not a religion. It is a frontier of the mind. There is great confusion about the difference between parapsychological work and popular occultism. As writers and as psychics we, the authors, do not believe ESP is demonic. We believe that children suffer their own private hells, and that through the knowledge and guidance of parents and teachers, children can develop healthy minds and healthy bodies. We wish to provide help in eliminating some of the problems and fears parents may be faced with, to help in understanding what is happening in a child's psychic experiences. Your child may be tuned into a channel you cannot see or hear. But if he or she is rebuked or scoffed at, irreparable damage may result. As a result many children withdraw into themselves.

In this book, a number of revolutionary ideas are evolved, based on ongoing research conducted by co-author Dr. Alex Tanous. It may challenge the public and the medical and related professions to demand more research to substantiate the theory that many childhood problems are due to psychic experiences that have gone unrecognized or unheeded. For the last several years parents have been asking Dr. Tanous how they can know if their child is psychic and what they can do to help develop or nurture this ability. This primer provides some answers.

In his lectures, Harold Sherman, author of *How to Make ESP Work for You*, asks an intriguing question: "How many of you know enough about the mechanisms of your car motor to be able to fix it if some little thing goes wrong on the road, so you can get on to a service station for repairs?"[1] Usually about 60 percent of the people in the audience raise their hands. The question then posed is: "Now let me ask you another question. You are each walking around with the most wonderful, sensitized instrument in the world inside your head—your own mind—upon which you have relied for everything that you have accomplished to date. Not only that, but your whole future happiness and success is likewise dependent upon the functioning of your mind. This being true, how many of you can tell me how your mind operates?"[2] From coast to coast, Sherman attests, not one hand has ever been raised. The important message he conveys following the no-show of hands is that perhaps it is time we all devote a few minutes of each day to the idea of learning about our own minds in order to operate them efficiently and effectively. Sherman, one of the pioneers in the field of ESP, strongly feels that how you think determines not only *what* but also *how* you are. It also determines how you respond to others and how they respond to you.

One of the main purposes of this book is to help you understand the mechanics of a child's mind and how the child's psychic abilities may be utilized for his or her future happiness. Many intelligent men and women have been greatly misguided by the quantity of misinformation in this field, and it is our wish that the methods and experiences included in these pages can serve as safe guideposts to you. As adults, you can also utilize your own innate psychic abilities in your everyday life. For example, a salesman walks into an office or encounters a group of people and realizes psychically, by telepathy or other means, that the proposal he wishes to present would not be accepted at this meeting. He then changes his course of action to work it into a more appropriate time when his presentation will be successful. Through *psychometry*—by shaking and touching hands—he may be able to sense the same thing.

Psychic experiences are useless unless they are applied to someone's development and success. By helping a child develop his psychic awareness his future is given a helping hand. Let's look at an amazing example cited by Harold Sherman—one that may well have saved his life:

I was in my room on the second floor of our family home. . . .
This room faced west, the sun was setting, it was growing dark. I was at my typewriter, and I got up, as I had done hundreds of times before, to turn on the electric light. As I reached for the switch, a voice in my inner ear, not a voice that I heard externally, said: *"Don't turn on the light."*

This was such an unexpected and eerie command that I hesitated, wondering why I should get such an impression. Unable to go against this impulse, I returned to my desk and typed for perhaps ten minutes longer, till it grew so dark that I just had to turn on the light.

But once more, as I fixed my attention on the electric light bulb, with my hand on the switch, the voice within repeated its warning: *"Don't turn on the light!"*

At almost the same instant, someone ran up to the porch downstairs and began banging the door and ringing the bell. I went downstairs without turning on the light and was confronted by a lineman, who said: "Don't turn on the light! There's a high-voltage wire down across your line outside!"[3]

In the previous ten minutes the lineman had been running from home to home to warn people not to turn their lights on. The strength of the lineman's thoughts had reached Harold Sherman's mind before his arrival.

What does this story have to do with psychic abilities and a child's future? Let's look at another example from Mr. Sherman: Guests who had been visiting with the Shermans left around midnight and discovered that their car had been broken into and a newly purchased suit had been stolen. Sherman had begun to put to use some of the information he had garnered about utilizing one's psychic abilities and decided to make a psychic suggestion to his subconscious: "No one will attempt to steal anything of mine but that I will be made aware of the theft in time to prevent it!" He repeated this again and again and then gave it no further conscious thought.

More than a year later, when Sherman was working in New York as editor of the *Savings Bank Journal*, he was asked by the publisher to remain for dinner to discuss a business matter. Just as he was about to leave, he had an impulse to put a copy of the current issue of the *Journal* into the inside pocket of his overcoat.

He didn't need the copy but obeyed his instinct. His overcoat was gray and nondescript, resembling many others that hung on the coatrack in the restaurant where he and his boss were dining. As the two men engaged in conversation during the meal, Sherman was suddenly hit with the thought: "Quick. That man has your overcoat." Although he consciously realized that an embarrassing situation would result if he accused any person of taking his coat and was wrong, Sherman's feeling was too strong to be dismissed. He looked toward the clothing rack just as a man removed a coat from it and started toward the cashier's counter. Sherman jumped up and weaved through the tables. Reaching the cashier's desk just as the man was buttoning the coat, Sherman said, "I beg your pardon, sir. I believe you have my overcoat." The man denied it, whereupon Sherman turned open the coat lapels, exposing the *Savings Bank Journal* in the pocket. The man apologized profusely, saying that the coat resembled his own. He gave it to Sherman, then took a few steps toward the clothing rack, as if he was about to get his own coat. Then suddenly he made a dash for the door and ran out of the restaurant. The manager, upon learning of the incident, told Sherman that six overcoats had been stolen in the previous two days.

Acting on an intuitive level stimulated by an earlier psychic suggestion that he had given himself, Sherman was able to prevent the theft of his coat. His unconscious mind, sensing he was approaching a time when his coat would be stolen, sent out the impulse to put the copy of the *Journal* in his coat pocket. It is important, too, to remember that Sherman had hung his coat many times on many clothing racks in many other restaurants without any cause for alarm that it might be stolen. Sherman explains:

I had not the slightest concern regarding my overcoat on this occasion, but the instant that this man, intent on stealing it, *touched* my coat, even though I was in the midst of conversation with Mr. Harrison, my Extra Sensory faculties got through to me with a definite warning! . . . Thomas Edison is credited with having said: "Man is only using one-tenth of one percent of his mental capabilities." It is undeniable that man has not, as yet, begun to sound the depths and potentialities of his own consciousness. Most certainly, few of us have developed sufficient control over our Extra Sensory faculties to be able to depend upon their added guidance and protection in our everyday lives.[4]

Today we cannot imagine anything that mankind will not ultimately discover. If we set our minds to a certain task, it can be accomplished. If in our mind's eye we search long enough for a solution, we will find it. Then, if we *will* it strongly enough, it will take place—when the timing is right. Just to "think" something is an act of creation! We hope that the parents and teachers who read this book will wish to help develop their children's CPE (Creative Perceptive Energy). With acceptance and understanding, parents can use the native psychic abilities of their children in a creative manner to round out their lives.

Regardless of the number of psychic experiences a child has, the same principle applies: *All psychic experiences should be utilized to integrate the child with his environment.* A child's psychic ability should be used to make him a "holistic" individual, to bring out his creativity so that he can use *all* of his talents to succeed. Parents and teachers alike can help a child accept his Creative Perceptive Energy by accepting it as a natural gift that can be enhanced through the ESP testing programs outlined in this book.

We are not urging parents to turn their children into fortune-tellers or to encourage them to make psychic predictions. Our aim is to help parents recognize that psychic experiences do take place and to help them accept these experiences as signs of a natural aptitude. One important point to keep in mind is that children with psychic abilities are creative individuals. When they are able to visualize what they want to achieve, they can achieve it. Helping a child to recognize his or her psychic experiences is like opening a door to a creative imagination.

This book brings you the experimental and test work of the late Dr. Alex Tanous and the comprehensive research of Katherine Fair Donnelly, both well versed in psychic matters. Dr. Tanous taught parapsychology at the University of Southern Maine. For many years, he worked with groups and families regarding psychic experiences. In the group process, adults talked about their heretofore unexplained experiences. In the family process, children were encouraged to talk about dreams, imaginary playmates, or any other psychic experiences they had. The purpose was to share what had happened to them so that they would realize that others, too, had similar experiences. This led both parent and child to the awareness that they were not "crazy," abnormal, or psychologically disturbed and contributed to their peace of mind.

In addition to teaching, Dr. Tanous displayed extraordinary psychic abilities and was an integral part of important scientific experiments conducted at the American Society for Psychical Research in New York with Dr. Karlis Osis. He also participated in experimental tests with Dr. Wilbur Franklin of Kent State University, Dr. A. R. G. Owen of New Horizon Institute, Dr. Robert Miller in Atlanta, and doctors at Columbia Presbyterian Hospital in New York. In Toronto, he was the subject of research on brain waves and psychic phenomena conducted by Dr. Joel Whitton, M.D.

Dr. Tanous earned numerous degrees, including an M.A. in philosophy, an M.A. in sacred sciences, an M.S.Ed. in counseling, and a doctor of divinity. Dr. Tanous was a certified school psychologist for the state of Massachusetts and a resident counselor at

Fordham University, and he taught at St. John's University, Manhattan College, St. Anselm's, and Anna Marie College. He also taught ESP at Thornton Academy in Saco, Maine, one of the first high schools to give such a course for credit.

The co-author of this book, Katherine Fair Donnelly, is an alumna of Southern Methodist University and was a journalist in Texas, thus establishing the background for her future work as a columnist, book reviewer, and author of many books, including *The Guidebook to ESP and Psychic Wonders*.

Katherine Donnelly's interest in psychic matters began after many psychic experiences of her own, one of which was a prophetic dream that she believes may have saved her life. Her quest to understand more of these psychic experiences led her to experts in the psychic field, both in America and abroad. Among these were Professor W. C. Tenhaeff, former director of the Parapsychology Institute at the State University of Utrecht in Holland; the president and principal of the College of Psychic Studies in London; Paul Beard and Ruby Yeatman; the highly respected sensitive Eileen J. Garrett (then also president of the Parapsychology Foundation in New York); the famed psychic healer Olga Worrall of the New Life Clinic in Maryland; and many other internationally known psychic investigators.

Because of her exposure to the "greats" in this field, Ms. Donnelly has been able to integrate her analytical ability and research with the experiments, tests, and findings of Dr. Tanous in an effort to help children in need of understanding.

Part One

Guidance for Parents and Teachers

One

Knowing What Is Psychic

Almost everyone has heard of America's Smithsonian Institution. When that organization lends its name to a project, we know that a stamp of approval has been granted by an authoritative source.

In 1976, the Smithsonian sponsored the first traveling exhibit on psychic phenomena. It was presented to the public as an educational program. The exhibit offered examples of psychic phenomena with introductory comments written by Dr. Margaret Mead, the noted anthropologist, lecturer, and author, in hopes of clarifying psychic research. Dr. Mead wrote: "The whole history of scientific advancement is full of scientists investigating phenomena that 'the establishment' did not believe were there."

If the Smithsonian Institution feels the time is right to present to adults explanations of what psychic matters are all about, wouldn't it seem fair for adults to explain them to children?

The principal psychic terms that will be used in this book are *telepathy*, *clairvoyance*, and *precognition*. Psychic experiences (sometimes referred to as *psi*) can involve one or more of these three.

Telepathy is the sending of mental messages or thoughts of any kind from one person to another without the apparent use of the physical senses. This has also been called *thought transference*. The important thing to remember here is that Person A is aware of Person B's thoughts at the moment Person B is thinking them.

Suppose we look at some factual examples of how telepathy works:

A girl of eight who lived in Maine had written to her friend in New York of an upcoming trip. She and her family were leaving the following week for a visit to Disney World in Orlando, Florida. The girl in New York had written a similar letter to her friend to say that *she* was going to Disney World. However, neither of the letters was delivered prior to departure. While in Disney World, the girl from New York had been thinking about the girl from Maine when to their mutual amazement, they met on the monorail! When they returned home, each found a letter waiting, telling of the vacation plans.

What purpose was gained in this telepathic communication? We see here that a message through normal channels—the postal service—did not succeed. Instead, from some other source of the mind, the girls were able to communicate their vacation plans and they met on the monorail in Disney World! Can you imagine what the odds are on such a meeting?

A ten-year-old Massachusetts boy was despondent because his best friend, Reuben, had recently moved to California. The child asked his mother if he could telephone Reuben. His mother agreed. As they went to pick up the receiver, the telephone rang. It was Reuben at the other end saying he had been thinking of his friend and had decided to call.

Here we see that the young ten-year-old missed his friend as much as his friend missed him. They needed to contact each other in some way. Telepathy was the impetus for the telephone call.

A young mother was driving in a car one morning with her six-year-old daughter. A traffic jam frustrated her, for she was in a hurry to get her daughter to school. Traffic was so snarled, it looked as if they would be there for some time. Waiting in the car, the mother thought, "How I would love to ram into that car and get traffic moving!" Her young daughter turned to her and said, "Mommy, if you do that, we will have an accident."

In this instance, the telepathic communication between the mother and daughter brought to full force the realization that, in the mood she was in, the mother might very well have had an accident. Her daughter's response to the telepathic communication alerted the mother to the possibility of accident if her impatience persisted.

Clairvoyance is the perception of distant events or people without the use of the five physical senses. This phenomenon consists of "seeing" the distant event simultaneously with its occurrence. Some investigators in this field state that clairvoyance can also include "seeing" the past as well as the future. To avoid confusion in terms, we will classify past events under *retrocognition* and future events under *precognition*. This is not to say, however, that clairvoyance does not take place in both those phenomena.

Let's look at some examples of clairvoyance:

While napping, a four-year-old boy dreamed that he saw his grandparents landing at the local airport. Upon awaking, he ran to tell his parents, but they had not been given any inkling of a possible visit from their relatives. Ignoring him, the parents started to dress the child to go out. Again he insisted that he had seen his grandparents and that his parents must wait for their phone call. The parents, thinking this utterly ridiculous, began to get ready to leave, against the child's protests. Just as they were ready to walk out, the phone rang. It was indeed the grandparents, calling from the airport: "We just got into town. We're only going to be here for a day and wanted to surprise you." But for the clairvoyant impression received by the young boy, the parents might have missed the grandparents' surprise call.

An eleven-year-old boy was reading in his apartment. Suddenly on the pages of the book he "saw" the image of the mother of his best friend. She had spilled boiling water on her arms and her hands and was screaming for help. The boy rushed to the woman's apartment, three floors above, and after he had applied his Boy Scout first aid, asked a neighbor to summon a doctor.

The above case is another example of how a psychic impression can provide a real help in everyday life. Many times in psychic experiences, stress and emotion seem to play a decisive role.

A doctor relates this story about his son. When he was five years old, the boy would always "know" five minutes before his father arrived home, whether late or on time. The child would run to his mother and announce, "I see Daddy. He is coming home now." And Daddy always showed up five minutes later.

This experience could be defined as clairvoyance in that the child "saw" Daddy coming home. However, it does not rule out the telepathic factor, that the boy may have received this form of communication from the father on his way home. In our research, we have found that many cases may be considered borderline and interpreted as either telepathic or clairvoyant. Some may combine both psychic forms. Whichever phenomena are operating, the resulting experiences are psychic in nature.

Let's look at another example of possible combined psychic talents at work: A young boy arrived home from school to discover that he had forgotten his keys. He began to think about his mother, but since she had gone shopping, he didn't know how to reach her. Suddenly, the mother "saw" the child at the door waiting and realized that he had forgotten his keys. She rushed to a telephone, called a neighbor who had an extra key, and told her to let her son into the house. Telepathically, the boy was thinking of his mother. She "saw" him waiting at the door. Either way, telepathically or clairvoyantly, a situation was resolved in a positive fashion.

Precognition is the foretelling or knowledge of an event that has not yet happened. In precognition, the person experiencing the event must have had no way of knowing of it in advance.

In the early evening of April 11, 1945, twelve-year-old Albert, living on the East Coast, was sitting in the living room, gazing into the fire. Suddenly he jumped to his feet and said, "Mother, the headlines in the paper tomorrow are going to say that President Franklin Delano Roosevelt is dead." Roosevelt was not known to be seriously ill at the time. The next afternoon a flash on the radio announced that he had just died of a massive stroke, and early evening newspapers throughout the United States issued extras telling of his death.

An interesting footnote to the above story is that Roosevelt had his fatal stroke while sitting before a burning fire in Warm Springs, Georgia.

This is a rather dramatic example of precognition, one in which the imminent death of a great world leader was foretold. We shall now turn to some that are less dramatic but equally interesting.

A father and his son had planned to go fishing the next day. At five in the morning, the father woke the son up to get ready to go. The boy excitedly told his father of a dream he had: "I dreamed we were sitting in a boat fishing and that a twenty-five-pound salmon at the end of my hook tried to pull me overboard." The father laughed and replied, "If you get a twenty-five-pound salmon, it will be a prizewinner. No fisherman has ever caught one that size in this water." They arrived at the fishing place at seven-thirty, and after some time, having caught nothing, were about to leave. As the son picked up his fishing rod, he felt it being pulled with a great force. Together, the father and son landed the fish, a twenty-five-pound salmon, which made the front page of the local newspaper the next day.

This psychic experience may have taught the boy and his father to pay attention to such dreams in the future. By doing so, the knowledge that information of a positive nature can be gained may prove invaluable in future endeavors. Graham Greene has attributed many of his successful novels to dreams that provided solutions to seemingly insurmountable obstacles.

Perhaps the young boy in the story above was apprehensive about the contemplated fishing trip with his father. In the sleep state, a marvelous solution occurred to allay any such anxieties: the landing of a twenty-five-pound salmon! Did the desire to fulfill his dream lead the boy to divine where to find the twenty-five-pound salmon? Or did he truly see a future event? In any case, the experience demonstrates the usefulness of calling on the unconscious to take over during sleep while the conscious mind is relaxing.

A significant number of children's psychic experiences are related to family members and friends, whose well-being is often the subject matter of a child's experience. The case below provides a good example:

Fourteen-year-old Helen dreamed that her favorite teacher was in a car collision while en route to school and was rushed to the hospital by ambulance. The day after this dream, Helen, along with the other students in class, waited for the arrival of their teacher. A substitute teacher appeared and announced to the class that the teacher had been in a car accident that morning and had been taken to the hospital.

This psychic experience may have served a useful purpose by preparing Helen in advance for the shock of hearing that her favorite teacher had been in a car accident, thus perhaps buffering the initial impact of the reality. In such a way precognition may serve as a guide to future events in a child's life and as an aid in coping with life in general.

The psychic phenomenon known as *precognition* is very interesting: You predict future events, and they happen as predicted. Unfortunately, little can be done to change the course of these events. However, there have been cases when a forewarning has averted injury or possible death, as in the dramatic story told by Phyllis Morris in *Two Worlds*. During World War II, when Mrs. Morris and her small daughter were about to flee from Singapore to India by plane, the child tugged at her mother's skirt and cried out, "No, no, Mummy, don't go up in alleoplane. Alleoplane go bomb, bomb and fall in the water." The child repeatedly cried the same phrases over and over again, unnerving the mother. When another woman, seriously ill, approached Mrs. Morris, pleading for her place on the plane, she reluctantly agreed to give it to her. The plane bound for India crashed, and all on board were lost.

Parents should understand the necessity of learning to recognize the precognitive ability of their children and must not worry about its importance on the course of their lives. We cannot determine exactly how valid or important an experience is until events enlighten us. It is our belief that precognition is just one more link to the psychic reservoir and to the tapping of a child's creative abilities.

Premonition is an experience akin to precognition and can best be defined as a vague, uneasy feeling that "something" is going to happen, but the "something" provides no specific information. The impact, as a rule, is a sense of foreboding about events to come, whether minor or major. One might ask, then, what is the difference between precognition and premonition? In precognition, one has a definite knowledge of a course of events that will take place in the future; in premonition, one has a feeling of something impending, a forewarning that is not distinct. Both of these psychic experiences can occur in a waking or sleeping state.

Let's take a look at some examples of what might be considered premonitions:

A young mother felt uneasy about letting her child go to school that morning. However, she dressed the boy and put him on the bus but could not shake off her strange feeling. Shortly after, she received a telephone message that the bus had been in an accident but that her son was not seriously harmed.

In precognition, while some experiences warn of impending danger, others serve to offer guidance or reassurance for the future. Premonitions do not appear to be as helpful as precognitions in averting oncoming events, usually because they do not provide enough information. However, the forceful impact of the "feeling" that "something" is not just right may cause one to take action.

Premonitions often deal with world events and celebrities. One such incident involved a four-year-old girl who was watching television with her family when Mahatma Gandhi appeared on the screen. "Mommy, the man is crying." The mother turned to the child and assured her he was not. The child persisted, "Sad man, sad man, crying." Gandhi died three days later.

Because of the vast number of premonitions that deal with natural or man-made disasters, a Premonitions Bureau was established in London in the 1950s; in 1968 it was followed by one in New York. (A detailed description of the purpose and activities of the Premonitions Bureau can be found in Chapter 4.)

The opposite of precognition is *retrocognition*, "seeing" the past without having any knowledge of it. Parapsychologist and psychoanalyst Dr. Nandor Fodor believed that Robert Graves, the novelist and historian, was able to go back into the past and "see" events that had taken place and that his uncanny ability to ferret out information from the past might well be attributed to retrocognition. Taylor Caldwell, the American novelist, may have had a similar talent.

Very little research has been conducted on retrocognition. The interested reader is referred to E. Douglas Dean's article "Precognition and Retrocognition" in *Psychic Exploration: A Challenge for Science*, edited by J. White and E. Mitchell.

A possible example of retrocognition, triggered by another psychic talent, *psychometry*, is given below:

A young man of twenty-two was found dead in his apartment. No clues were found by the police, although homicide was suspected. A year later, a girl of fourteen moved into the apartment with her parents. Without realizing that she was standing where the body had been found, she told her parents about the murder of the young man and the details of the crime. In learning later from neighbors that the crime had actually occurred more than a year before, the parents contacted the police, who found the information new and very helpful.

Psychometry is a channel for picking up information about a person or events, whether past, present, or future, from touching an inanimate object or from sensing its presence through energies emanated. Some individuals are able to tell the history of objects by touching them. Others can find missing objects and, more important, missing people.

The following experience of a seven-year-old girl shows signs of psychometry:

Tina was going through some objects her mother had put away in a box. Intrigued by various pieces of jewelry and religious articles, the girl began to pull out a few of them. She was particularly attracted by red rosary beads, and, turning to her older sister, she said, "This is Grandma's rosary. She had it with her because she loved it." The child proceeded to recount details about where, how, and when the grandmother had died. The sister ran to tell their mother, who returned with her to where Tina was still holding the red beads. Upon examination of the rosary, the mother confirmed that it had indeed been the grandmother's favorite. She was astounded that the child, who knew nothing of the events, could relate such minute details about the grandmother's death.

Again we must remember that, as in *all* of the psychic processes, psychometry may involve more than one psychic form. Thus, in feeling or touching the object, the child may have been experiencing clairvoyance of the past—retrocognition—probably set off by the psychometric touching of the rosary beads.

Dowsing, a psychic talent used throughout the world, is considered by many to be similar to psychometry. Here, the inanimate object, such as a forked stick, pendulum, tree twig, or elongated V-shaped prong, is used to detect the presence of minerals, underground water, lost objects, etc. The operator holds the forked end of the twig or dowsing tool close to his body, with the stem pointing forward and down. When he walks over a place where the sought-after water or mineral lies, the stem of the divining rod is pulled down. This may be attributed to the heightened psychic sensitivity of the diviner or to pure chance. Dowsing may be performed indoors, using similar instruments, placing, say, a pendulum over a map. The pendulum swings in a circle over the map and slowly stops over an area where whatever is being sought may be found.

Groups of dowsers meet all over the United States. At one such meeting a father asked his son to use a pendulum in an effort to locate a lost dog. When placing the pendulum over the map of the city, the boy saw it swing to a point and stop. The spot was then marked by the father, who called the police, who found the dog near the place on the map that the child had located through dowsing.

A former president of the American Society for Dowsing, John Shelley, was doing a radio show in Boston. To test the host, Steve Fredericks, who had never done any dowsing, Shelley hid a number of coins in the studio while Fredericks took a break. The listeners were told that the coins had been hidden. After the host returned, Shelley gave him a dowsing fork and asked him to start walking around the room. "When the fork dips," said Shelley, "you will know you are close to the coins." The skeptical host began to move about the studio. Suddenly, on air, he screamed out his startled response. He had found the coins where the fork had led him, hidden behind a picture on the wall.

A fourteen-year-old boy heard his father telling a neighbor that their well was polluted and that a new one had to be found. The boy, whose father had practiced dowsing from time to time, took a divining fork and started to dowse for water behind their house. To his astonishment, one hundred yards in back of the house, the wooden fork bent so that it broke. The boy marked the spot and called his father. After digging for less than two hours, they found a fresh source of water.

Many large professional firms use dowsers to find oil, water, etc. During the Korean War, the army had some of its soldiers study dowsing in an effort to detect mines. The efforts proved successful. Obviously if dowsing can be used to find lost objects, hidden water, and minerals, it can be a boon to mankind. Dowsing may serve as an exciting game to stimulate children's imagination and enhance their creativity.

We now arrive at what may be considered a paradox in psychic phenomena—*psychokinesis*, or PK. Psychokinesis is the influence or energy a person exerts upon an object without the use of physical energy, the moving of an object through mental power alone. Dramatic accounts of so-called PK have been given in radio, newspaper, and television reports of keys and silverware being bent, clocks and watches stopping or spinning, glassware flying about the home, etc. While many parapsychologists scoff at the idea of the mind controlling matter, others in the field take it seriously and are testing it in the laboratory, almost to the exclusion of other psychic phenomena.

Below is a simplified and condensed list of the various psychic terms and their relationship to the all-encompassing phrase *extrasensory perception*.

The sending of thoughts to another is TELEPATHY.
The visual perception of events or things is CLAIRVOYANCE.
Knowledge of the future is PRECOGNITION.
Picking up information by touching an object is PSYCHOMETRY.
Moving objects without physical exertion is PSYCHOKINESIS.
All are forms of ESP.[1]

Two
Colors and Their Importance

Colors fascinate children, for they live in a world of hues and tints. Although moving things—pull toys, balls, cars, and trains—are favorites of the youngest, the crayon box and finger paints have innumerable fans among the preschool and kindergarten sets. We never outgrow the love of color, and our possessions and hobbies reflect this attraction. It is not unremarkable, therefore, that color plays an important part in psychic life.

Since man first appeared on earth, he has considered colors to significant. In the Stone Age, red, ochre, and black were thought to have magical powers and were used in cave paintings of men hunting beasts. It was believed that painting an animal in those colors guaranteed the hunter success.

In historical times, the Egyptians painted sarcophagi in bright, vivid colors that were repeated inside the tombs where the bodies were laid to rest. It was believed that bright colors ensured the dead person's enjoyment of a happy afterlife. In ancient Greece and Rome, specific colors were given important designations. Purple and gold were used in the raiment of royalty. Green was the color of victory; white was for the pure and virginal young. In Greece, white was also believed to enhance healing. Doctors would prescribe white garb for their patients, which was supposed to help in the healing process.

In the medieval paintings of the Western world certain colors were used to depict various Christian themes: A red rose or pomegranate was the symbol of the Virgin Mary. The celestial heavens were generally painted gold. Jesus was usually depicted in either a purple (royal) or a white (pure) robe. Other white symbols of Jesus were the lamb, the lily, and the wafer used at the Last Supper. The Holy Spirit was generally shown as a white dove.

Closer to modern times, the founding fathers of the United States chose the colors red, white, and blue for the American flag because of emotional impact: Red represented strength and fortitude, white signified purity, and blue heralded truth and virtue. The stars were used to represent the United States as a new constellation in the galaxy of nations. The stripes represented the original thirteen colonies.

In the twentieth century, many hospital rooms are yellow and pale green because of the healing and soothing effects of these colors. No one would dream of putting an ill and feverish patient in a bright red room, because bright red represents fervor and feverish activity. This is an example of the psychological impact of color, and psychology, being a science of the mind, includes psychic phenomena.

By their very nature, colors are psychic as well as psychological in impact. Stress and emotion can induce psychic experiences. It is our belief that colors evoke psychic experiences in much the same way.

The following interpretations of colors are the results of research conducted over the past fifteen years with more than two thousand people, both children and adults.

Colors can generally be divided into two categories: those that are lively and uplifting and those that are depressing and life-less. Among the lively colors, pink and red represent love and human affection but also vigorous activity. Orange falls close to those two colors, with a similar emotional impact: It is indicative of a forceful ego. Yellow represents helpfulness and sensitivity and is also conducive to artistic activities such as writing, painting, playing musical instruments, etc. Blue represents balance and evenness, while green signifies deep emotional feeling and carries weighty thoughts. Gold and silver are symbolic of the spiritual nature of man. Light brown and beige are indicative of idealism and lofty goals, such as helping people in various ways. Purple has healing power; when wearing that color one generally has a sense of well-being.

As pointed out above, the darker colors are considered depressing. Dark brown tends to lower the spirits and may produce an attitude more conservative than usual. Gray, for the most part, suggests lethargy, nonproductivity, or some unhappiness. Black and midnight blue denote sadness, depression, and despondency. White, the blending of all colors, has an awesome mystical appeal to many people.

An interesting aspect of our research indicated that individuals showing a preference for the colors blue, white, yellow, and red seemed to have more psychic experiences than those who preferred other colors.

While there are other interpretations as to the meaning of various colors, the above are reflections of our studies and observations and are offered simply as indicators. We are not recommending that parents and teachers become color experts overnight by reading a few pages. We are only suggesting that the parent or teacher be aware of the relation of color to a child's mood and to the moods of adults. You may benefit psychologically and psychically by observing the colors you choose.

During a parapsychology course in which these basic color concepts were defined, the people in the class were asked to indicate their reaction. We cite two of the many interesting responses:

"I am much more keenly aware of color now. It is very interesting to note the colors that my friends wear and how well they seem to reflect their moods. I noticed a heaviness in one friend's attitude for several weeks. She consistently wore a gray overblouse. Upon talking with her for a length of time, she revealed that her husband is leaving her for another woman." In perceiving her friend's mood, the woman was able to gain her confidence and help her in a time of distress.

"I find pastel colors make me feel happier. I have noticed if I find I am choosing a dark color, I can change my mind about the color and, in that way, change my mood and therefore control my life and what happens around me better and better." This student wants to be aware of her moods, to maintain a happy frame of mind, and will try to gear her moods in that direction through the use of color.

We believe the color guidelines given here will also provide some background to help put you in tune with your child and provide you with a handle on his or her behavior. It is not our intent to make you overly concerned if your child chooses to wear a dark color. Rather, it is our hope that you will simply become aware of your child's mood when he or she wears dark shades. A child who continues to wear dark colors for a long period of time may have a problem that needs your attention. Usually the predominant color a child chooses is symbolic of his or her mood.

Let's look at the observations of a young mother:

"My four-year-old daughter loves green and pink. These colors have been her favorites since she could verbalize at around eleven months. My son (age two) has always systematically removed all the purple crayons he could find and put them with his 'special' toys." Since the young son chose to put the purple crayons with his favorite toys, his mother perceived that he was happy with the color and wanted it near him. Had the boy discarded the purple crayons, it would have had another meaning, which his mother would infer from the other colors he selected. In general, the mother noticed that her children were happy and healthy.

Through psychic awareness, children, too, are able to perceive moods activated by colors. Here is a story told by the mother of a seven-year-old girl:

"When my daughter Anne-Marie was getting ready for school one morning, I had put out some clothes for her to wear, among which was a blue sweater. Blue was one of her favorite colors, and I thought she might enjoy what I had selected. However, she put the blue sweater away and instead pulled out a gray sweater that had been a gift to her from an aunt. Usually in the mornings her friend Christine came by to meet her, and they would go to school together. This morning, however, I saw that Anne-Marie was getting ready to leave for school without Christine, and I asked her why this was so. My daughter said Christine was not going to school that day and had to stay home because she thought Christine had fallen and 'hurt her arm last night.' Moments later, the telephone rang. It was Christine's mother to say that Christine had fallen and broken her arm and would not be going to school that day."

In the above case, since Anne-Marie had had no verbal communication, the choice of gray indicated sadness stemming from the psychic impression she received that her friend Christine was ill. By choosing a color different from her favorite, the daughter made her mother aware that the color had meaning for her.

Our research reveals countless instances where color seems to trigger psychic experience. Telepathy may communicate the impression that something is wrong: *I know something is wrong, but*

I don't know what it is. In clairvoyance, the impression is received: *I know Johnny has a toothache because I "see" it.* The child sees the color. Through it a connection is made, and he receives the impression that something is wrong.

In *The Paranormal Perception of Color*, Dr. Yvonne Duplessis has this to say regarding feeling and color:

> To go one step further: even a passing feeling arising in us can cause the appearance of a color. Thus a headache or a toothache evokes for certain persons the color blue or red, the different shades of which make it possible to describe them to others with greater facility than with words. The astonishing fact is, as we shall see later, that such persons can sometimes express in colors not only the impressions of their own deeply felt sensitivity but also the impressions of others. Once again, colors serve as symbols of the deep zones of people's psychism.

She also holds that "certain persons can experience impressions which seem to be premonitory and signal the beginning of a disease." Dr. Duplessis goes on to state that color investigations are "difficult to conduct because adults, fearing ridicule (let us repeat), when questioned on this subject, often refuse to answer, and even more so in regard to persons capable of receiving telepathic or premonitory impressions."

In recent years school blackboards have been changed to green, again creating a better mood for children through color. In school and other areas of social contact, a child may not be able to express his color preference. Therefore, it is important that at home the child be allowed to choose the color he likes. Let him either wear it or play with it, for the color he chooses will affect not only his day but also that of the people around him. In being permitted to utilize his color sensing, the child is unconsciously influencing his own psychic vibrations. He is creating an atmosphere in which he can perform better in the classroom, at play, or wherever he is. Such a psychic awareness on the part of parents and teachers can help open up the child's mind to channels of creativity. Colors indicate the child's negative and positive moods, reflecting how he feels at the time. With understanding, the child's attitude toward creativity can be changed from nonproductive to truly productive.

A boy of twelve had been doing poorly in his studies. He appeared to have few friends, and he seemed somewhat withdrawn. The boy's family had a small income. As a result, he inherited many of his older brothers' clothes—garments that had survived years of wear and tear and were mostly of dark colors. One day his parents bought him a yellow sweater. When they gave it to him, he blurted out a dream he had had of getting just such a sweater. The child was elated, and his entire personality seemed to change. Something had clicked. His teachers were aware of this, and he became more at home in the classroom. His schoolwork improved. He began to develop better. He made more friends.

Something within this child said, "If I get this color, my life is going to change for the better." In the dream he was receiving a yellow sweater, which classifies the experience as precognitive. And in this instance, the parents may have telepathically received the boy's nonverbalized plea for a change in his life by way of a yellow sweater.

It should be noted that precognition doesn't necessarily mean you must dream of a disaster such as a plane crash. It can also mean that you know something is wrong with you and that if X happens, your life will be improved in the future. This awareness comes from your basic or elementary self. While the aftereffect may be psychological, it was the "psychic self" in the above story that brought about the solution. Whether we label this experience psychic or psychological, certainly something developed in a positive manner as a result of the boy's receiving the yellow sweater. Here again we have an example of how the psychic and the psychological may work hand in hand, for, like psychology, psychic phenomena are related to the science of the mind.

The following excuses may be made to explain one's lack of certain colors:

"I have a limited wardrobe."

"Light colors show the dirt too quickly."

"I went shopping and couldn't find a thing in the color I wanted and had to settle for another color."

"Where I work I would stand out like a sore thumb if I wore bright colors."

"Nothing else was clean, so I wore my brown dress to the party."

"With prices the way they are today, you don't shop for color, you shop for value."

There may not be an abundance of the color a child is seeking, but most likely he can find some article of that color. If the child can find nothing in the color he wants to wear, he may take the color he needs to express his mood from a box of crayons. If he can't find anything that will enable him to express himself satisfactorily through color, he may very well dream about a yellow sweater!

Dreams that are in color indicate that the dream is psychic in nature. (Psychic dreams will be dealt with at greater length in Chapter 4.) Parents should listen carefully to their children when they describe their dreams as being in color. A color dream that is remembered as being *very vivid* is almost certainly a psychic dream related to experiences that have happened or are yet to occur.

The use of various colors helps to develop the right side of the brain—the child's intuition, sensitivity, and creative vision. Bright colors, in particular red, orange, and yellow, appear to be those most conducive to creativity. They spur the right side of the brain to action, thus contributing to a child's holistic development. On the other hand, dark colors seem to act as a depressant and tend to block a child's creativity.

Holistic simply means that the right side (the intuition) and the left side (the logic) of the brain are balanced, and a total mental balance is being created. The child's vision and intuition can be put to practical use. His creative ability will help him in whatever he is doing. Children go through many moods and will want to wear different colors to suit those moods. The important thing is to allow the child's creative ability to operate in a balanced manner and not to stifle that ability.

During the early life of a child, parents should use their intuition to give the child the right colors. When the child is around two years old, his parents should give him some say in choosing the colors he wants to wear. By that time, children are able to distinguish between the colors they like and those they dislike. If the closet is full of clothing that doesn't appeal to the child, an inexpensive accessory in his preferred color can help create the balance he needs. If his least favorite colors are forced on a child, they can upset his balance and harm his ability to achieve. Given a choice of colors, a child's expression is limitless.

Teachers, along with parents, can participate in helping a child express himself through color either with crayons or finger paints. Children can be told "We are going to do a painting today; pick your own colors." Let the child select his own crayons, and don't make it obvious that you are testing him. It is also important to remember that in this type of test not only is the color important, but so too the form and shape of what is drawn. The age level of children being tested with color crayons should begin in the home at around two or three and can be continued into later years either in the classroom or at home. The experiment should be conducted in the morning to see what colors the child selects; his choice can act as a mood barometer. If, for example, a child uses a crayon of the same color for several days, especially black, the teacher or parent can try to determine the child's underlying problem. The more sensitive a child becomes to color the more sensitive he will become to sound and sight—and eventually more sensitive to psychic abilities.

Dr. Gerald Jampolsky, noted psychiatrist and author, tells of testing a young girl who had a great ability to distinguish between colors when she was blindfolded but whose ability disappeared when her parents told her not to do this because "It is bad." The girl became withdrawn and later refused to learn. This type of situation occurs all too frequently, primarily because parents are fearful of social ostracism or of conflict with their religious beliefs. However, Dr. Jampolsky believes that all children, whether sighted or blind, can be taught to tell one color from another by developing their psychic abilities. In testing blind children, it has been observed that their ability to perceive color helps them to "see" their environment. Tests conducted in California by Dr. Jampolsky proved that blind psychic children can distinguish red from blue and black from white. In the same tests conducted among sighted psychic children, the youngsters, when blindfolded, were able to discern red from blue and black from white.

For example, in Dr. Jampolsky's tests for color perception, red and black cards were used. The children were told red would "feel" hot and black would "feel" cool. Some of the children did experience those particular sensations. Others experienced sensations of tingling, roughness, smoothness, etc. Still others indicated the image that came to their mind upon touch. A high degree of accuracy was found in distinguishing the black from the red cards. (Additional details concerning this type of testing are found in Part III.)

Dr. Yvonne Duplessis relates the story of a blind woman, Mrs. Leila Heyn, who was trained to "see" with her hands. Sensations associated with color seemed to predominate. She was able to "see" flowers in a vase. In experiments with René Maublanc, professor of philosophy and author of *Une éducation paroptique* (*A Paroptic Education*), Mrs. Heyn was able to "see" the color on jonquils. After four and a half months of further exercises, her color "vision" was such that she was able to select dresses from her closet! What a marvelous thing if blind children could be taught psychically to "see" colors and thus enhance their lives in so very many ways.

When a child states that he sees colorations around a person's head or body, he is perceiving what is known as the "aura." The human aura consists of many colors and shades, depending upon the emotion and health of the individual it surrounds. It is seen as many vibrant bands of color, somewhat misty, encircling the person's head and body. The first band projects about one-half inch from the body. A second auric band extends approximately three to four inches, and a third band about eight to ten inches from the body. It is in this last band that many claim to see the pulsating shape or colors, the "aura." It is the second band, or inner aura, that seems to contain the most brilliant colors or, conversely, in the case of illness or depression, the darkest and most muted colors. Many individuals capable of seeing the aura have compared it to heat waves like those that rise from boiling water or from the hot pavement.

In *The Paranormal Perception of Color*, Dr. Yvonne Duplessis states that one of the purposes of those gifted in seeing the human aura is to aid physicians and criminologists. The ability to "read" the aura has been helpful to physicians who have called on such gifted individuals to determine illness by the colorations they "see" in the auras of patients. Similarly, police have sought assistance from aura-reading psychics who work as investigative aides to help solve crimes.

If your child says he sees lights emanating from a person's head, he probably does see them, and you should not scoff or make fun of him or threaten him with punishment for telling "lies" about seeing lights or colors. We cannot urge you enough to treat all psychic experiences in a natural way as they are just that—natural!

Don't worry about interpretations. Just be aware that when a child says he is seeing colors in this fashion, he very likely is and that he will expect you to explain to him what is happening. By being knowledgeable, you can provide your child with an answer that will enable him to go forward with his everyday activities rather than retreat into a shell because he thinks he is different.

If we try to recall the first time we ever saw a rainbow, we may well remember the awesome sight of so many beautiful colors and asking what caused a rainbow to occur. We may ask now about the bewildering mystery of detecting colors through psychic means. Let us look to the wisdom of William Wordsworth:

My heart leaps up when I behold
A Rainbow in the sky:
So was it when my life began;
So is it now I am a man;
So be it when I shall grow old . . .
The child is father of the man.

Three

Imaginary
Playmates

Would you hit your child with a baseball bat? Would you hurl your child against a brick wall? Would you hold your child's hands over an open fire? Nothing is more deplorable than the battering of children. Yet many parents and teachers batter children emotionally and seem completely unaware of the tragic effect of their lack of understanding.

There are many ways to hurt a child. When a child announces that he has a "playmate" whom he can see but you cannot, is he slapped and told to stop lying? Is he laughed at by his parents and rebuked by his teachers?

A child who has suffered a broken wrist can be taken to a hospital. The wrist can be X-rayed, put into a cast to help it mend, and attended to by a physician. A child who has suffered an emotional break has an injury that is not visible, one that can continue to fester unrecognized until many years later. This type of child abuse can be even more severe than physical battering. The child with the broken wrist can see the cast that has been applied to help the fracture mend. Soon, he becomes aware that the wrist is healing, and ultimately he will see the cast being removed—and the problem being solved. No such relief is in store for the child who has suffered the heartbreak and emotional scars of disbelief and rebuke.

The imaginary playmate gives rise to impatience and disbelief among parents and teachers. Episodes involving imaginary playmates can be emotionally disruptive for a child, and for his parents and teachers. Parents have no conception of what their child is going through and tell him no one is there, that what he has experienced is nonexistent, and that he should forget about it. The child may be put through years of torture because his parents and teachers don't believe him. He begins to suppress his feelings, afraid to speak for fear of ridicule. Since neither his parents nor his teachers comprehend what he is experiencing, he is given little in the way of help or guidance and flounders alone, haunted by thoughts that he is different and unacceptable to his peers. Worse, he cannot understand why.

Imaginary playmates generally fall into several categories. They may be:

1. "Real"—The child actually sees the playmate, talks to him, can describe him, and is convinced of his existence.
2. "Imaginary"—The child wants to believe he has this playmate and makes him up, even though he knows the playmate does not exist.
3. Produced by telepathic communication.
4. Either a sprite or a spirit that finds children unusually receptive.
5. A duplication of the child, a condition sometimes referred to as *dual consciousness*.
6. Due to an out-of-body or bilocation experience.

Correspondence from Dr. Berthold Eric Schwarz, prominent psychiatrist and consultant at the Brain Wave Laboratory of Essex

County Hospital Center in New Jersey, provided us with further clarification of the imaginary playmate:

In *Parent-Child Telepathy*, I did go into "imaginary" playmates, which, as you know, is a normal, everyday, healthy experience for many children in growing up. At that time of life the ability to separate reality from fantasy is not fully developed—if that is the correct way of looking at it—and the imaginary playmate serves a definite need for the child's maturation and emotional development. Naturally, if it goes on for any great period of time it indicates other things.

Dr. Schwarz goes on:

As indicated, an imaginary playmate serves an everyday function in the development of the child who has this experience. It is a widespread type of event, and as the psychiatrist can learn much by observing the child in his play viz. the objects chosen, the plot, the outcome, etc., he can also learn much by understanding the nature of the child's communication with the imaginary playmate. It can be quite revealing of the child's needs, feelings, personality, and character structure. The difference between the "real imaginary" and the "imaginary imaginary" playmate would depend on having all the data at hand. The subjective reality is there, yet the healthy child would know at heart that it is an "imaginary imaginary" playmate. However, as you well know, there are cases in literature where the real and the imaginary merged and it would be impossible to determine how much of one, or how much of the other goes into it. It is usually a blend. One can speculate though that the child who has this going on is in a receptive frame of mind—in a trancelike state, or altered state of consciousness—and would also be open to all kinds of subtle telepathic influences, as described in *Parent-Child Telepathy* and many other publications by a variety of interested psychic researchers. We can only guess at the purpose when we have sufficient data.

A professional student at the University of Southern Maine relates the following story: "My young son is five now and in school. But last year he was four and had two 'imaginary' playmates. He was home alone most of the time with only me and the television. His playmates' names were Broom and Apple. I would ask more about them, and he would tell me stories about them, for example, that they were going shopping with us or that they were playing games with him. They have disappeared now that he goes to school and has human friends. He doesn't even mention them anymore."

When the child was home without human companions of his own age, he turned to imaginary playmates to fulfill his need for companionship. When the child went to school and developed friendships with children of his own age, there was no longer any need for the imaginary playmates, and they disappeared.

Another example is that of a young boy who traveled with his parents to South America. The boy's imaginary playmate accompanied them on the trip, and he and his playmate had animated conversation on the way. Observing that their son was somewhat silent on the return flight home, the parents asked him where his playmate was. The child replied, "I left him in South America because that is where he was from and he wanted to stay there."

Many children have imaginary playmates of foreign origin. This may be explained in part by astral projection or out-of-body experiences, during which either the child or the imaginary playmate may visit a foreign country and be transported back in a relatively short time. Another explanation could be the television screen, on which a child sees foreign countries and people of foreign extraction right in his living room. Then, too, stories of other lands stimulate the child's mind to bring forth an exotic or foreign imaginary playmate. In the case described above, the boy's imaginary playmate was from South America, and the child may have felt that the playmate should be repatriated to his native country. Therefore, when the imaginary playmate said he wanted to stay in South America, the boy consented.

Can more than one person see the imaginary playmate? While it is rare, there are instances on record of this having taken place. A striking story is told by Olga Worrall, the famed healer, who was conducting services at the New Life Church of the Mount Washington United Methodist Church in Baltimore, Maryland:

During the summer months, occasionally traveling ministers going to Washington, D.C., stop by at the New Life Clinic. About a year ago two such ministers with their wives and children attended the New Life Clinic service. I saw five children as I stood in the pulpit (I was preaching that Thursday). One little girl in particular attracted my attention. She appeared to be about seven or eight years old. She wore a huge bow in her hair—quite old-fashioned, I thought. After the service was over, the children ran out to play, and I saw this little girl playing with the other four children. The parents asked if I would have lunch with them and I suggested we could all go someplace to eat. They said, "That won't be necessary, we have our trailer . . . and we'll have sandwiches. . . ."

So we all piled into the rear end of this little trailer truck—it was a cute thing—and four children joined us. I asked, "Where is the fifth one?" They said, "What do you mean the fifth one?" I said, "Why, the fifth child you had in church with you today." So I described the little girl. I said that she was playing right out there. One of the couple's daughters, seven years old, spoke up and said, "Oh yes, that was Margaret." They looked at her with unbelief, then she added, "Margaret comes with us all the time. She's my best friend." She knew this little girl and was in full agreement that I saw Margaret.

Her mother asked, "Where did Margaret go?" The child answered, "When Margaret has to go away, she disappears." Then they began to question the child, "How long have you known Margaret?" And the child said, "Oh, I've known her a long time. She always comes to me when I go to sleep at night." I'll tell you I was shaken because to me, Margaret was just as real as that little girl who sees Margaret and knows her as her best friend.[1]

The above testimony is not that of a hysterical individual. It was related by a woman who has received worldwide recognition for her healing ability. The Johns Hopkins Medical School, after receiving a grant from the Department of Health, Education and Welfare in 1977, invited her to lecture on the spiritual healing process.

Mrs. Laura F. Knipe, executive secretary of the American Society for Psychical Research, relates the following experience from her childhood: "When I was about three or four years old, I remember that a little girlfriend and I had two imaginary playmates whom we both could see. We used to set the table for four because they were coming to tea, and when they came, we would talk for hours. We were both able to talk to our two playmates and used to play together in the backyard. Members of our family used to smile and say, 'Oh, have your friends come for tea?'"

While one of the little girls may well have influenced the other, this would appear to be an instance in which each child saw the playmate of the other and thereby could give greater credence to their existence. Here, too, is a situation in which parents and other family members helped a child by accepting her imaginary playmates as part of her everyday existence and by not scoffing at or belittling the child's belief.

Dr. Tanous recalls two of his childhood experiences with playmates. In one, he played with a group of children in Maine who shared the same imaginary playmate, an American Indian: "We used to get feathers from the chickens. Then we whooped and danced and climbed trees and did all sorts of things with our 'Indian Chief.'" The friends not only saw the playmate but knew the Indian's name as well."

The second experience shows that imaginary playmates need not be children but can be animals, too: "When I was very young, we were poor. Our neighbors all had dogs, but my family couldn't afford to support an animal, although I always wanted one. One day, Fido—my imaginary dog—appeared. He was a beautiful basset hound. We played together. I would feed him imaginary food. He followed me to school, slept in my room at night. We were the best of pals."

Helen Stefanik, head operating nurse at New York Hospital for over thirty years, tells of the many imaginary playmates who came to visit her as a child, seeking assistance and instruction in their schooling: "When I was around seven or eight years old, there were quite a few playmates who came to see me in the early afternoon, and they remained well after dinner. They were all girls, and I would help them with their lessons and teach them." In later life, as head operating nurse, Helen was responsible for teaching and training the younger nurses. Her ability to do this may have stemmed from her early experiences with the imaginary playmates. On the other hand, her imaginary playmates might have been a form of precognition of what her later duties in life were to be. When asked how long the playmates lasted and when they disappeared, Helen replied thoughtfully: "They left when I was around ten or eleven. I guess I just outgrew them."

When do imaginary playmates appear and how long do they last in the life of a child? The answer to this question varies. Generally, parents become aware of their child's imaginary playmate when the child is about two or three (at the age when children are able to tell about it), and the playmate's existence continues up until the child's ninth or tenth year. Some playmates disappear after the child goes to school. In other instances, the playmate appears when the child first goes to school and may continue until the child is ten or eleven. The need of the child plays the most important role in the length of the imaginary playmate's existence. Children may have a particular playmate for a certain length of time; by the time they are eight or so, their sense of logic takes over. Children then realize that the playmates are indeed imaginary and are no longer needed.

In the following story we not only see that a playmate can appear for just a brief period of time, but we also are made aware of the role telepathy can play in evoking an imaginary playmate. Dr. Berthold Schwarz told us of an intriguing experience he had. When visiting his mother in her Montclair, New Jersey, home he was casually introduced to her new pet crow. His mother fed it bread, and the crow would sit on her hand or shoulder. When his mother stepped outside, the crow cawed and flew to her. Dr. Schwarz thought his children would have great fun speaking to the crow. The next day he returned to the seashore, where his wife and children were staying, and was told by his wife that his daughter Lisa had been talking to an imaginary crow on a neighbor's fence at the very time he had been at his mother's home the day before. There was no way the family could have known about the bird.

Schwarz says, "Yes, Lisa spoke only on that one occasion to

the crow, and that's what made it unique, and it was such an odd event at Mantoloking, where she was at the time, that my wife took note of the whole thing and was quite surprised, as I recall, when I told her about the strange crow experience at Mother's. Unless the need existed and dovetailed with the telepathic event, I doubt very much if the imaginary playmate would have persisted. For example, if the parents, by verbal, or better yet, by nonverbal stimulation give feedback to the child in such a situation, it would naturally encourage it, and such a fostered imaginary playmate would be the case."

Not all "visitations" by imaginary playmates herald pleasant experiences. A mother reported: "My young son told us that he had an illness and was not going to live." The child was indeed terminally ill, but the parents had never told him. They asked the boy how he knew. His reply was: "Another little boy came and told me not to be afraid, that we would be playing together soon and that the pain would go away." The pain did go away; the child did foresee his own future. The imaginary playmate was a comfort to this boy in a very real and poignant way.

Perhaps the boy's parents were unable to repress their nonverbal thoughts and concern for the boy's well-being, and through the telepathic impression received, the child brought forth another little boy as a playmate to help him, since his parents could not. Researchers in this field have found that at the time of death, patients may have out-of-body experiences during which friendly spirits come to help them bridge the gap between this life and the afterlife. This has been well documented by Dr. Karlis Osis and Dr. Erlendur Haraldsson in their book *At the Hour of Death*, by Dr. Raymond Moody, author of *Life After Life*, and by many others.

What exactly are spirits and sprites? One point of emphasis is that they are not harmful. A spirit can be described as an entity or energy that has the ability to make itself known. The period in which it lived may be observed by its mode of dress and speech. Many parapsychologists and psychic researchers claim that spirits are probably well-adjusted discarnate beings who actually want to help the living, whom they contact in order to impart information.

Sprites are mischievous but playful ghosts, again not harmful. Dr. Berthold Schwarz states: "I have cases in my files of children who have seen—for lack of a better term—a ghost sitting in an easy chair, and then told the parent or other interested person about it and that checked in with experiences of their own. It doesn't mean it was a real ghost, it all could have been telepathic, but it did tie in with a preexistent reality of some order."

It is next to impossible to give clear-cut evidence that an imaginary playmate is indeed a spirit or sprite. Many other hypotheses and alternatives have been offered, such as that of telepathic communication, indicated above by Dr. Schwarz, in which case it is felt that thoughts can appear as what seems to be a spirit. Let's look at some examples that show the fine lines involved here:

A boy of five informed his parents that "Grandpa" told him he was going to have a baby sister soon. For several years the parents had been trying without success to have a child. Grandpa was dead, and the parents were upset by their child's story. However, within the year, a baby daughter was born, and their young son's prediction came true. What then do we have here: spirits, sprites, or telepathic thought? Was it possible that the grandfather at some time prior to his death could have conveyed the desire for a granddaughter? In their hope to have another child, did the parents yearn for a girl because their parent had wished it? Through telepathy, the young son may have received this thought and evoked the image of a baby sister. As to knowing in advance that a child would be born and that it would indeed be a girl, this is an example of precognition on the part of the child or the spirit of the grandfather. In any event, it was a psychic experience, and one that had a happy ending.

Athena Drewes, a research parapsychologist affiliated with the Division of Parapsychology and Psychophysics at Maimonides Medical Center, New York City, tells of one child whose great-grandmother had died before she was born and who used the name of the great-grandmother as the name of her imaginary playmate as well as for one of her dolls, though the family had never mentioned the great-grandmother's name to the child. When her parents asked why she had selected that name for her playmate, the child replied, "Because she told me that was her name."

Most children with imaginary playmates obtain their names from the playmates themselves. In the above case, the child may have had an experience of retrocognition. It is also conceivable that the child may have received a telepathic communication from one of her parents as to the name of the grandparent. For example, one parent might have had a thought such as "I wish her great-grandmother Anne had lived to see my child." In picking up the thought, the child then could have produced a playmate bearing the great-grandmother's name, as if to say "Don't be concerned; she is here and can see me." Another possibility is that the child or the playmate may have been in contact with the spirit of the great-grandmother. Or it could have been sheer coincidence.

Vera R. Webster, science editor for a major publishing firm, tells of a younger sister who was adopted at a very early age after her mother had died. When the little sister was two years old, she was sitting on the front porch one day and was overheard talking to someone. Queried about whom she was speaking to, the child replied, "To my mother." When told that her mother was inside the house in the kitchen, the girl replied, "No, I mean to my mother up in heaven." She did not know she had been adopted, yet insisted she was speaking to her mother in heaven.

Here again we have the possibility that some form of communication with discarnate spirits may have taken place or that a telepathic thought may have been transmitted either through the older sister or one of the parents. The young child could then have brought forth the imaginary playmate of her real mother, who had passed away. In this instance, the latter would appear to be the more likely explanation, although it does not rule out other possibilities.

Dr. Jampolsky states, "Children with high psychic ability generally have imaginary playmates that they treat as real. These playmates can be a duplicate of themselves." This is sometimes referred to as *dual consciousness*. For example, a six-year-old girl, the eldest of four children, tells of an imaginary twin sister, even though she had two real sisters and a brother. Apparently a need existed to bring forth a twin sister, who may well have been a duplicate of the girl. Further inquiry revealed that the girl recalled that her parents and grandparents had wished the first child to be a boy. She also remembered a traumatic incident in which a grandmother had taken her to a barber shop to have her hair cut off so that she resembled a boy. While no verbal statements may have been made to the child about the strong desire for her to have been a boy, these thoughts may have moved the child to create a "twin sister" who was the girl she wanted to be, and who could exist without the heartache of knowing that her grandparents craved a grandson.

Dr. Schwarz emphasizes the importance of telepathy in the needs of children and adults:

How many things go on in life that are totally ignored or relatively meaningless until the telepathic hypothesis is considered and used? And then, Eureka! The pieces of the puzzle fall into place and a pattern and meaning is clearly discerned. Many telepathic events are answers to silent questions, or complement urgent needs, or negatively considered, supply sensible but highly adaptable (even if they are disagreeable) reactions. They serve to maintain one's emotional and physiological equilibrium.[2]

Another hypothesis to explain the reality of the playmate is that time and space are transcended. Either the playmate or the child is present in another place. This is known as *bilocation*—being in two spots at the same time. Parents cannot always check on the reality of the imaginary playmate. If a child says he is playing with "Sousoi," and Sousoi is in China, the name may be very unfamiliar to the parent, but Sousoi can be very real indeed. In this instance the child may have broken time and space. If the child needs a playmate other than those offered in daily life—a grandparent, a sister, a new identity—it comes forth as an imaginary playmate because there is a real need for it in the child's life. Imaginary playmates serve a purpose or they wouldn't be there!

In determining the real need of a child for his or her imaginary playmate, let's look at the following recollection of a young student: "At the age of eight, I had a high fever and hallucinations, dreams, fantasies, or whatever. When able to walk, I went to the doctor and the illness was diagnosed as rheumatic fever. The fantasies were of *Mrs. Wiggs of the Cabbage Patch* characters. Mrs. Wiggs was forever talking to me. The conversations were pleasant, and her figure was always present in my mind. She was as big as I was. She never left me. After the fever subsided, my mother told me I really had a vivid imagination. Although she laughed and said I was getting better, she did not belittle or make a judgment. I am sure she was happy and relieved that the illness was over and that now she could care for her other three children and my father. I had rheumatic fever three more times, each time in the spring of the year, and each time the same Mrs. Wiggs and the garden dominated my mind. The spring of my twelfth year, I had my tonsils removed and no more rheumatic fever."

It didn't make any difference, apparently, if the playmate was real, imaginary, a spirit, or a sprite. Mrs. Wiggs came through at a vital time in this child's life and continued to do so in times of stress, perhaps even helping to save her life. Certainly there is no greater need, and with the recognition of the importance of the child's need, the imaginary playmate should be fostered rather than hindered, accepted rather than rejected, welcomed rather than denied. As the child in the above story indicates, "Mrs. Wiggs never left me," and in another instance states, "Now she [the mother] could care for her other three children and my father." The underlying fear of the child that her mother might not be present at all times during her recurring illness but might instead have to tend to the needs of her other children and husband could well have evoked the helpful and caring Mrs. Wiggs, who never left her.

It is difficult to distinguish between a "real" imaginary playmate and a made-up one, as indicated by Dr. Schwarz. However, it is not of primary importance *which* it is so long as the needs of the child are met. Our purpose is simply to make parents aware of what imaginary playmates are and to help them understand what their child is seeing and experiencing. It is extremely important that parents not try to squelch the imaginary playmate or shame their child. The key is to *listen* to the child, be *sympathetic* to him, and not make a big issue out of it—to *accept* it as natural.

Parents can try to determine the identity of their child's imaginary playmate by asking the child the name of the playmate, what he looks like, what he is wearing, what he says. These questions should be asked casually, just as you might ask the child what he has watched on television in the afternoon. If the name of the playmate is familiar to you, like the name of the great-grandparent in the story above, then you can assume it is a "real" imaginary playmate. However, simply because it cannot be related to reality doesn't necessarily mean the playmate is *not* real, as in the case of Sousoi above. Sousoi came from China and actually existed as far as the child was concerned even though the name was totally unfamiliar to the parents.

In this way, parents can try to determine the psychic ability of their child. If the imaginary playmate is "real," this is a psychic manifestation from the child through telepathy or other means. If the imaginary playmate is "made up," it is a manifestation of the child's storytelling abilities and should not be stifled. Many journalists had such active imaginations as children. Of course, if it can be determined that the imaginary playmate is either a sprite or a spirit, it is a manifestation of the child's psychic awareness and is not to be feared. What it is is not important to the child, as long as the playmate serves his or her need in a healthy fashion.

If the imaginary playmate gives a child instructions to do something evil or destructive, this could indicate the child's need of psychiatric assistance. Steps should then be taken to seek help in this area. It is of extreme importance that parents and teachers do not tell a child that the imaginary playmate is nonexistent. This would shock the child and jar his reason, altering his life and causing him to withdraw.

The imaginary playmate—it cannot be emphasized enough—is a real need of the child, and his belief in it should not be challenged or destroyed. It's like Santa Claus: Let the child find out for him or herself through logic!

In closing this chapter, we would like to relate a touching experience that occurred during a lecture to an audience of two thousand at the Civic Center in Augusta, Maine, when a question was directed to Dr. Tanous: "A boy of about ten was sitting in the front row with his father. During the question-and-answer period, he asked me, 'Can you tell me when I am going to die?' I responded, 'Young man, that is the wrong question to ask. What you should ask is Will I live long enough to accomplish what I want to do? and the answer is yes. But you don't believe me, do you? Well, let me ask you a question that your father knows nothing about. You still have your imaginary playmate, don't you?' And the kid looked up and softly said, 'Yes.' I asked, 'Could you tell us his name?' and he did. The father then exclaimed, 'But you never told me that,' to which the child replied, 'But, Dad, you wouldn't understand.'"

You wouldn't understand. This would appear to be the unspoken plea of many children who have had such psychic experiences as imaginary playmates. We must try to understand.

Four

Psychic
Dreams

*I have heard say of thee, that thou canst understand
a dream to interpret it.*

—GENESIS 41:15

After the pharaoh's dream about the fat and
lean kine, and the good and the thin ears
of corn, Joseph was summoned for help.
Joseph's interpretation of the pharaoh's dreams and his sage
advice saved Egypt from a great famine. It is probable that the
precognitive dreams were recorded because of the importance of
the figures involved, the ruler of Egypt and the hero of the Jews.
We can only be grateful that the record was kept.

The subject of dreaming has been studied since ancient times,
but *why* we dream is still a mystery. More easily explained is why
we have particular types of dreams.

Let's take a look at the role dreams and their interpretation have
played in human history. Man's interest in dreams began with
primitive cultures and the early civilizations. Dream interpretation played an important role in everyday life. Dreams were generally considered to be either visitations of the gods or prophetic

pronouncements. Indeed, some cultures believed dreams to be the wanderings of the human spirit released in the sleeping state.

Probably the earliest practitioners of dream interpretation were the druids of Celtic Britain and Gaul. The druids believed that certain dreams of their priests were prophetic declarations. Most important decisions awaited the interpretation of such dreams. The old Irish bards who may have witnessed some of the druidic predictions have sung songs in praise of such dream interpretations. In the Middle East, the Jews as well as the Egyptians have held dreams in great regard. The Old Testament is a wealthy storehouse of psychic phenomena as well as dreams and their interpretations.

When Abimelech was visited by God in a dream, the purpose was to solve the problems he was having with his wife. The dreams of Jacob and his ladder envisaged the gateway to heaven. Joseph's interpretations of the pharaoh's dreams are considered biblical classics.

In the New Testament, many dreams that deal directly with the birth and infancy of Jesus are recorded. In particular there are those of Joseph, Mary's husband, who was told on one occasion that her child was the Son of God and on a second that he should take them to Egypt for safety. The dreams of the Wise Men about avoiding Herod are most interesting because of their precognitive nature: the murder of the innocents.

Plato and Aristotle believed a man's soul left his body while he slept. They believed that in the sleeping state the soul wandered around, gathering knowledge of the past, present, or future. Interestingly, both of these philosophers warned of overindulgence in drink and food before sleeping. They claimed such intemperance created "unlawful dreams," i.e., nightmares.

In the Roman era, we can consider three dreams as classics: Calpurnia's portentous dream about the murder of her husband,

Julius Caesar; the Emperor Augustus's dream of the birth of Jesus as the Prince of Peace; and the warning dream of Pontius Pilate's wife "to have nothing to do with that just man, for I have suffered many things this day in a dream because of him."

With the development of science and rationalism in the eighteenth and nineteenth centuries, dreams were ignored as unworthy of interest or speculation. However, some literary and artistic men stand out as exceptions: Edgar Allan Poe, William Blake, Robert Louis Stevenson, Voltaire, Shelley, Tolstoy, Coleridge. These men claimed to rely on dreams and visions to aid their artistic and literary endeavors.

With the coming of the twentieth century, interest in dreams was once again aroused. Dr. Sigmund Freud, in his *Interpretation of Dreams* (1900), was one of the first scientists to list dreams as an important mental activity. Freud considered dreams to hold keys to the discovery of the makeup of the individual. A Freudian axiom became "You can know a man by his dreams." He asserted that dreams were essential to an understanding of man and were certainly worthy of careful and exhaustive scientific study. Another twentieth-century scientist who studied dreams and their interpretations was Dr. Carl Jung, who postulated that the outstanding feature of psychic dreams was that they were generally in color and left a vivid impression on the dreamer. He divided psychic dreams from "ordinary, trivial dreams," claiming that psychic dreams came from "the deeper self—the real person." Dr. Jung felt that ordinary dreams came from "the trivial self—the common task." His definition of the psychic dream was:

It is a little hidden door in the psyche, opening into that cosmic night which was psyche long before there was any ego consciousness, and which will remain psyche no matter how far our ego consciousness may extend.... All consciousness separates, but in dreams we put on the likeness of that more universal, truer, more eternal man dwelling in the darkness of primordial night. There it is still the whole, and the whole is in him, indistinguishable from nature and bare of all egohood. Out of these all-uniting depths arises the dream, be it never so infantile, never so grotesque, never so immoral.[1]

To parents who prefer a more simplified definition we offer the following: Dreams are a mental activity that always take place during sleep. They are made up of many images, scenes, or thoughts that are always expressed in terms of sight rather than hearing or smelling. Dreams are rarely brought about by sensual impressions.

It is our contention that external stimuli rarely determine the content or form of the psychic dream. Furthermore, we believe that dreams can be divided primarily into three categories: *psychic, wish fulfillment*, and *nightmares*. A fourth category is put forth by many psychoanalysts who state that certain dreams—those including tunnels, suffocation, narrow passageways, and the like—are due to the trauma of birth and that such dreams serve as release mechanisms.

What is the purpose of dreams? Dreams are many things. They enlighten you about the nature of men and events. They tell you what problems the psyche is encountering. They also tell you what the collective unconscious has been thinking since the dawn of man. Dreams can be telepathic, clairvoyant, precognitive, retrocognitive, or astral in nature. In other words, they can tell the dreamer what other people are thinking through thought or sight, or through going into the past, and particularly they can tell of future events. Precognitive dreams are those most likely to occur in the realm of psychic dreams.

Dreams fall into several categories.

One of the outstanding features of a *psychic dream*—far more so than that of an ordinary dream—is the striking impact on the dreamer upon awakening. The dreamer can remember the most minute details. The dream was *vivid*. Most psychic dreams are in color and appear to deal with telepathy, clairvoyance, or precognitive events. In some rare cases, they indicate retrocognition, in which the dreamer had knowledge of events in the past that he would have no conscious way of knowing. (Astral phenomena will be discussed at length in the next chapter.)

The *wish-fulfillment dream* is usually fleeting in nature and is generally in black and white. An outstanding feature is that the dreamer achieves a goal he desires and has not been able to attain. The wish-fulfillment dream can include sexual desires, career goals, gourmet satisfactions, sports achievement, etc.

The world of *nightmares* encompasses frightening dreams, generally in black and white, with shadows or shades of gray. They are horrendous experiences expressed in symbolic terms; nightmares are rarely, if ever, expressed in realistic terms. Many children between the ages of two and four experience nightmares, sometimes for long periods.

Let us enlarge upon the definitions of the various types of psychic dreams and give examples illustrating them.

A psychic dream may give exact details of what is going to happen, or it may be symbolic, as in the following case of precognition. A twelve-year-old girl had a Christmas dream in September concerning three candidates for the gubernatorial race in Maine. She was instructed to climb a ladder and put a football on top of the Christmas tree. If the football remained at the top of the tree, candidate Longley would win. If it fell to the left, another candidate would win. If it dropped to the right, the third candidate would be the winner. The girl took the football to the top of the tree, and it stayed there. When the election was held, Longley became the governor of Maine.

Using the above as an example of what a symbolic psychic dream might be, let's look at a psychic dream that is realistic and again precognitive. A ten-year-old dreams that she looks out a window and sees her brother being pulled out of the water. She sees a man trying to revive him with mouth-to-mouth resuscitation. She notices the blue color of the water, recalls how the man is dressed, and remembers other details vividly. Later, when the brother is actually pulled out of water and revived by a neighbor who gives the child mouth-to-mouth resuscitation, the events in the young girl's dream are repeated in reality.

In a symbolic dream, it is important to note that if a child is retentive enough, the dream will emphasize something he or she could be aware of, such as the football in the case of the young girl above. She had to be aware that if the football stayed at the top of the Christmas tree, something specific would occur: a cause-and-effect relationship.

Obviously all psychic dreams are not clear-cut. In many instances they appear either illogical or too garbled to interpret. When one also is aware of the fact that the conscious mind may distort or push aside what is welling up from the unconscious, the idea of trying to make sense of dream messages seems overwhelming. Nonetheless, interpretation is possible. In many cases the symbolism in a dream is the most effective way to convey a message that can be quickly grasped by adults who want to help the child and possibly by the child himself.

A Central Premonitions Registry was established, first in London and then in New York, in the hope that early warnings might provide information to aid authorities in dealing with possible disasters. For example, many people foresaw the 1966 landslide that demolished and buried a school in the Welsh coal-mining village of Aberfan. Among them was a young Aberfan schoolgirl who pleaded with her mother the day before the disaster to "let me tell you about my dream last night." The mother replied that she had no time to listen. The girl was insistent. "Mummy, you *must* listen. I dreamt I went to school and there was no school there. Something black had come down all over it." The next day the school was buried beneath the landslide.

Parents or teachers who wish to submit dreams or premonitions of disaster may write directly to the Central Premonitions Registry, P.O. Box 482, Times Square Station, New York, NY 10036. Robert Nelson, director of the registry, explains in *Parapsychology Review*:

> Each first-time writer receives a standard-response letter explaining the procedures for filing premonitions and instructions as to monitoring dreams for possibly psi-induced material. Upon request photocopies of predictions date-stamped "Registered C.P.R." are sent to the participants. Anyone who shows psi-talent by achieving a "hit," a close correspondence between a registered event and subsequent actual occurrence, or who relates highly detailed and significant past precognitive experiences, is sent a Psi Profile Questionnaire.

Since its beginning, contributors from twenty countries as well as thousands of people from every state have written to the registry, all happy in the knowledge that their predictions or premonitions are going to be taken seriously.

To further illustrate telepathic dreams, we have this: A boy of nine dreamed that his school chum was helping his family pack to move things into a new home. The next day he told his friend's parents about the dream and they were astonished; they had just decided the previous day to move to a new house. In his dream the young boy received the information telepathically.

A psychology student at Boston College whose husband was a

pilot in the Korean War had a dramatic telepathic dream. She had to prepare a term paper and could not decide what to write about. That night she dreamed that her husband was sitting at a table and writing a letter to her: "Dear Mary: I am writing you this letter just before I am off on my flight. I believe this is the last flight I am going to be on. Mary, I love you very much. . . . " It was quite a long letter. In her dream she also saw the airplane flying, then crash. She woke up with the dream's vividness and clarity still with her. She could remember the dream in minute detail. Mary decided that her dream would be the subject of her term paper, which she told her somewhat skeptical instructor. Three days later, she received a telegram from the government announcing that her husband was missing in action. Seven days later, on the day she was scheduled to turn in her term paper, the same letter from her husband that she had "seen" in her dream arrived in the mail. She photostated it, put it with the term paper, and turned it in.

While this dream certainly was telepathic in nature, it also can in part be classified as clairvoyant in that the student "saw" the letter in the dream, probably at the time it was being written. She may also have picked up either the telepathic fear her husband was experiencing about the flight, or the airplane crash in the dream may have been in part precognitive either on her part or on the part of her husband.

There are some in the parapsychological field who hold that the dreams of children are substantially different from those of adults. However, if dreams are basically either telepathic, clairvoyant, precognitive, or nightmares, and if they are presumably based on man's unconscious experiences from the very beginning of his life, why should there be any great differences? Adult dreams may be a little more sophisticated, but if they are based on experiences before they are born from the unconscious collective mind, as Jung propounds, then they must be essentially the same. Younger children may not be able to express themselves well enough to relate their dreams in great detail. However, by the time children are seven or eight, they should be able to do so.

A child should not be forced to share his dream. If he wants to discuss its contents, his parents should pay careful attention to those of his needs that may be revealed in the dream. However, they should not set themselves up as final authorities on dream interpretation. Children may be anxious to tell their dreams, dreams that may often be psychic in nature. Parents should not scoff at a dream's contents but might simply remark, "Oh, isn't that interesting! Well, let's see if it happens." If the dreamed-of event does occur, the child's parents might say in a casual tone, "You dreamed that and it happened, didn't it?" If the dream doesn't come true, the same matter-of-fact tone should be employed. Whichever the case, nothing should be made of the incident. At no time should parents let their children think that a precognitive dream is a special event; rather, it should be treated as an ordinary occurrence. What a child really wants is for his parents to listen and provide love, care, and concern.

Most readers of this book are not equipped to make dream interpretations. However, psychic dreams do seem to offer helpful clues, in that they are mainly identifable as being precognitive, telepathic, or clairvoyant. The ability to classify a dream is one step toward interpreting it. In many cases messages that may not be easily accepted in the waking state are received during dreams.

A dream that had a strong impact upon a young girl and the choice of her life's work is told by Athena Drewes, the managing editor of *Psi News*, who has written extensively and conducted research on ESP in relation to young children:

It was a Saturday night and beyond my bedtime. I was busy hurrying to finish reading the book *Ben-Hur*, which had been made into a movie that we would soon see. With only four pages left, my mother turned out my light against my protests, frustrating my efforts to finish the book. I was extremely angry before falling asleep. That night I dreamt of a car crash involving my family. I was the observer watching it all occur. I watched as the crash took place; then the scene shifted to my observing myself and my brother sitting in wheelchairs, unhurt, at the hospital, and watching my mother being wheeled in on a flat high stretcher. A type of stretcher I had never before seen or knew existed. I knew my mother was injured but my brother and I were not. One week later, these same scenes occurred in real life, exactly as dreamt, down to the last detail.

Athena tells of the indelible imprint the dream made: "As you can imagine, this had a strong impact on me and my life. As a result, I have pursued the fields of parapsychology and psychology with great interest and have since made both my professions."

Many times we are warned in dreams about impending danger. While problems may occasionally be averted by knowing the future, at other times the foretold event does take place, despite our dream-warnings.

An illustration of the latter is pointed up in a teenage student's dream of being in a car accident during a rainstorm. The next day in class at the University of Southern Maine, the student related the dream to her parapsychology instructor, who urged her not to ride in a car for one week. For the next week, the girl followed his advice scrupulously. One day later, she was walking when it suddenly began to pour. A car stopped at the curb, and a good friend of hers called, "Hurry and get in; you're going to get soaking wet." The response to jump into the car was so spontaneous and the relief of being out of the downpour such a comfort that the girl gave no thought to the dream. But just as her friend pulled the car out from the curb, a truck hit them. Neither Janice nor her friend was hurt, but the car she rode in *was* in an accident, during a rainstorm.

Another dream in which a warning was given even more specifically is that of a writer who dreamed in the month of October that she would be in an accident on February 8. During the fall and winter months she was extremely careful, and when February 8 arrived, she stayed home the entire day. At the end of the day, she was tremendously relieved, believing that her dream had been unfounded. However, the next day, on February 9, she was crossing a street. The sun was shining brightly on what she thought was a stream of water, but as she stepped on the shiny patch, she slipped and fractured an ankle. The water turned out to be ice.

What do we have here? Could it be that despite warnings, certain things seem to be preordained? Or, simply that the unconscious mind had not relayed to the conscious mind symbols that may have been lost in the dream? Perhaps some symbol that could have provided a clue that the accident would occur *after* February 8 had been present. Perhaps some other symbol may have clarified the ice situation. In many instances dreams are of a fleeting nature. The first reaction of the dreamer is to grasp the main symbols quickly, much as one would remember the outstanding impressions of a movie recently viewed. However, not *all* the details of a movie are remembered or thought to be significant!

Most children between the ages of two and four experience a series of nightmares. They may dream a monster is lurking in the bedroom, perhaps sitting on the bedpost or hovering above them ready to pounce. These creatures may take the form of lions, tigers, various kinds of birds, even dinosaurs or alligators.

Various theories have been put forth to explain the occurrence of nightmares. One theory holds that they are brought on by some startling or frightening event during the child's day. The "frightening event" could be an everyday occurrence, such as the barking of a dog or the sudden scream of a police siren. The breaking of a favorite toy can evoke harsh nightmares. Another theory holds that these nightmares may be induced by a child's feelings of guilt for some "bad" action that he was involved in during the day. Still another view holds that nightmares are brought on by the so-called "children's illnesses," which are particularly prevalent during the ages of two to four. There is some evidence that nightmares tend to increase during periods of physical illness. This may be especially true if the parents show overconcern for the child's well-being at such a time. Some doctors in the field caution that children may use nightmares to establish bedtime rituals, such as leaving the light on all night or sleeping in their parents' bed. Parents should not comfort a child in a manner they are not prepared to continue night after night, for many complications may arise as a result.

How, then, can parents handle their child's nightmare? When your child tells you that a tremendous alligator is on the floor and that he is afraid the animal is going to hop into bed with him, listen attentively. Express your concern and amazement that the alligator had the audacity to enter Johnny's room without being given Johnny's permission or yours. Direct your voice to the area the child has described, and in a firm tone address the "monster" in words such as "Just you get out of here, you alligator. You have no business being here, and Johnny wants you to leave. So I am telling you to get out and don't you come back here again." When you leave the room, if the child wishes to have a favorite toy remain with him, by all means allow him to have it. Assure the child that you will look in later to make sure the alligator got your message and will not come back to bother him.

Why is it a monster that appears in the child's nightmare in the first place? Why doesn't the nightmare repeat the actual experience? It is possible that telepathy plays a part in this. If the parent is momentarily startled by the sound of a barking dog, or a loud police siren, that instant of concern may be conveyed telepathically to the child. Because of the anxiety experienced, the end result may be a nightmare, for very young children cannot relate to everyday experiences on an adult level, cannot divide reality from fantasy. We must remember that young children spend a good deal of time listening to or watching on TV plays and stories in which animals and giants are involved. Because of this, everyday startling occurrences may be translated into dreams of hobgoblins and monsters.

These events may trigger other types of anxieties. Children soon become aware that their parents can go away for periods of time and do not come back the instant they are wanted, whereas in earlier childhood crying often evoked a quick response. The ages of two to four are generally a painful growing-up period. The sudden realization that a parent is not always present to tend to his or her needs may provoke the appearance of the monster in the child's nightmare.

Let's take the example of a child who has watched a TV program about a mother and father bear who leave their cub alone in the cave. Moments later, the cub is threatened by the appearance of a cougar. The problem presented in the program would very likely be resolved by the return of the mother or father in the nick of time to save the cub. But they have not returned in time to save the young program-watcher the anxiety of wondering if his parents would come to the rescue if monsters were to threaten him. Nightmare monsters may simply be the child's plea to the parents to "please be here to save me from harm." The process of growing up and becoming aware that parents are not immediately on call can give rise to a child's apprehension that his mommy or daddy might be away during a time of real need. This anxiety takes hold during the sleeping state and manifests itself in the form of the threatening monsters in nightmares.

In dealing with a child's nightmare, parents should express genuine concern and indicate that they are on the child's side, that they are on hand to make sure the monsters will not bother him, and that their presence and action will rid the child's room of these bothersome interlopers.

We are reminded of a friend who is an avid dreamer but who often dislikes the way his dreams end. He has a marvelous way of handling the problem: He goes back to sleep and *redreams the ending*! Perhaps our friend has a real solution hidden in his unusual aptitude: If parents hold their child, comfort him, and appreciate his fear, perhaps the monsters can indeed be sent packing—and new dreams will have new endings!

Five

Out-of-Body Experiences

What if you slept?
And what if, in your sleep, you dreamed?
And what if, in your dream, you went to heaven and
*   there plucked a strange and beautiful flower?*
And what if, when you awoke, you had the flower in your
*   hand?*
Ah, what then?

—SAMUEL COLERIDGE

One such extraordinary experience, which was recorded in *Fate* magazine in September 1963, happened to Carol Hales of Quartz Hill, California. Carol saw a vision within the branches of a large tree in her yard. The face of her friend Jaime Palmer appeared, appealing for aid and expressing an urgent need.

Carol rushed to telephone Jaime but received no answer. A bad storm had come up, and her friend's house was ten miles away. Carol searched her mind desperately for some way to extend help to the friend whose image had appeared in the tree branches. Then, lying on her bed, Carol experienced a sense of calm and relief. She felt as if she were rising and drifting easily and comfortably from her body, from her room, from her home. She seemed to be drifting in a calm, "aware of the wild shriek and the tremendous blow of the wind yet untouched by it." While in this "drifting" state, Carol found herself at the balcony leading to Jaime's bedroom. Upon entering, she saw her friend lying almost unconscious on the bed, obviously very ill. Carol drifted slowly down to the garden below. The storm had quieted. "I recall touching an orange tree and tightening my fingers about a piece of green foliage," she reports.

When the dream ended, Carol awoke, and in her hand was the piece of green foliage! There were no orange trees anywhere near her home. Convinced this was not a dream, and spurred by this realization and her waking desire to assure the well-being of her friend Jaime, Carol telephoned another friend and physician, Dr. Marion J. Dakin, who, with her nurse, went immediately to Jaime's home. Receiving no response to their knock, they called out. There was still no response. Then they checked all the doors. Fortunately, a side door had been left open. Entering, they found Jaime on the bed desperately in need of help. She was rushed to the hospital in Santa Monica, where emergency surgery was performed and a large gallstone removed. Later Jaime Palmer was told that if the operation had been delayed, the gallstone would have ruptured the intestinal wall, endangering her life. When the attack began, she remembered, she thought of contacting Carol for help but didn't want to worry her needlessly.

Carol Hales had an experience she could not accept as merely a dream: "Where did I get the foliage from an orange tree? And how did I know of Jaime's desperate need?" If it wasn't a dream, what was it?

The idea that one can float away from or outside of the body is a frightening thought to those unaware of the potential benefits of the experience. The fear of "something spooky," "something different," "something scary" is the reaction of many. "You don't really believe that kind of stuff" is a response heard many times from intelligent people who feel that because they can't see a thing they have reason enough to believe it can't be there. In *Man, Visible and Invisible*, the theosophist C. W. Leadbeater says: "It is one of the commonest of our mistakes to consider that the limit of our power of perception is also the limit of all that there is to perceive."

The very term "out-of-body experience" can be alarming unless one comprehends that there is also a "return-to-body" experience. Our purpose is to help alleviate fears and to explain that children, as well as adults, have out-of-body experiences. Listed below are some of the purposes served by this type of experience.

The out-of-body experience (OBE) has been a means of locating lost objects and, even more important, lost people!

The OBE can provide definite help, as in the above-mentioned case of Carol. The OBE also helps in study, for example, in finding important information in a book.

For children with inquiring minds, the OBE provides a means of travel during sleep.

For others, the OBE provides relaxation, and those who have experienced it state they feel renewed energy upon awakening.

During an illness, the spirit in an OBE energizes the body and assists in the healing process.

It simply may be that the mind wants to hook into the "collective unconscious."

These may sound like extremely unusual reasons for out-of-body experiences, but who is to say they are not germane? They may be the workings of an imaginative and adventuresome mind, for the mind can produce extraordinary effects, both real and imaginary. Originally, man went out to roam, hunting for days, weeks, sometimes months at a time for sustenance. Perhaps the mind now seeks sustenance in a similar way.

The out-of-body experience is the traveling of the spirit through space, leaving the physical body behind at rest or asleep. *Astral projection*, or astral flight, is the same as OBE. The psyche is able to wander freely, returning later to the sleeping or resting body. Another term frequently mentioned in connection with out-of-body experiences is *bilocation*, the state of being physically projected into two places at one time.

Parapsychologists and researchers offer many hypotheses concerning the out-of-body phenomenon. Although the argument about what name to give this experience continues, the OBE is psychic in nature no matter what we choose to call it.

While in the OBE state, telepathy, clairvoyance, and precognition may occur. The OBE may take place during sleep, while in the "twilight zone," or in the waking state. In most cases it is spontaneous and comes on without the individual realizing it and also without his or her having any say in the ultimate destination involved in the experience. In rare instances it can be self-induced. Dr. Karlis Osis states: "From my experience and research, I have found that most OBEs occur in the waking state. They also occur in the twilight state and in the sleeping state."

Our concern is to convey that some part of the consciousness leaves the body and travels to another place before returning. That place can be anywhere, a site never visited before as well as one that the subject already knows.

In the following dramatic experience, we can see the practical use of the OBE:

"I remember an out-of-body experience I had when I was four

years old. I was playing on a swing in our backyard. It was the kind of swing that had lots of hanging ropes and bars. Suddenly, I got caught in one of the ropes. It was twisted around my neck. I couldn't breathe or talk. Suddenly, I felt myself leave my body and float over to the back porch window. There I called to my mother, who was in the kitchen. She heard my cry for help but could not see me. She rushed out into the backyard and saw what was happening to me. She untangled me from the rope and held me in her arms. I watched from the porch. After I had been freed, I returned to my body."

We have given valid reasons for teaching children how to cope with out-of-body experiences and have stated their value in relaxation, the finding of lost objects, the regaining of strength, and help in studies. How much more important can any experience be than saving the life of a child?

In another case, a six-year-old girl told her parents she had floated out of her body to Paris, visiting many of the city's out-of-the-way streets, which she described in great detail. Her parents laughed at the child's vivid imagination. Nonetheless, the child persisted in her claim that she had been to Paris. A year later, the parents decided to take their daughter on a trip overseas and included Paris in their itinerary. While in Paris, they became lost in an unfamiliar area. No matter which way they turned, they could not find their way out of the maze of little streets. At this point the child spoke up, stating that she knew the way. The girl repeated what she had told her parents earlier: that she had floated out of her body and had seen these streets before. She proceeded to lead her lost parents out of the maze and on to their destination.

In this case, the out-of-body experience was an aid in solving the dilemma of being lost in a strange city. Let's take a look at how an OBE served to locate a missing object.

During a discussion period in a parapsychology classroom,

a woman related an incident concerning her father, who had recently passed away. Not knowing where he kept his will, the woman went to her father's home to search for the document but to no avail. She returned to her own home and despairingly told her husband about her inability to find the will. Her young son, who overheard the conversation, made no comment. However, the next morning he ran to his mother to tell her that in the night he had "left his body" and gone to visit "Grandpa's house." He told her that he floated out the window of his own bedroom, over to his grandfather's house, and into the kitchen. There the boy floated up toward the ceiling and landed on the top shelf of a cupboard, where he saw a metal box. Inside the box he saw two envelopes, one inside the other. The inner envelope contained the will for which his mother had been searching.

The mother, although sophisticated in psychic matters, was stunned. She immediately took the child to her father's home and asked him to point to the place where he had seen the box. The boy pointed to the top shelf, which the mother couldn't see from where she was standing. Climbing a ladder, she found the metal box her son had described. Inside were the two envelopes containing the will.

A study conducted among students at the University of Southern Maine revealed that many of them, as children, had experienced a feeling that they were "drifting away" from their body or out of their body, floating or looking down at happenings below. Many who had experienced such "driftings" remembered being reluctant to speak about their experiences to family members or friends. They did not wish to be considered strange or different; they were afraid of being ridiculed.

One unusual story concerned a student who, as a young girl, had been waiting for friends on the corner of her town's main street in late afternoon when suddenly every person evaporated.

She could see no one. The streets were empty, but all the buildings were standing. She looked around and realized that she was floating in the air and could see the tops of the buildings. The girl told her friends about it, and "they really had a good laugh." Later she told adult members of her family, who "just looked at me strangely."

Years after her unusual experience the girl, now a married woman, was taken to the hospital. Two days later a nurse said to her, "Were you lucky last night!" Then, the girl remembered: "I had 'gone away' and I was above myself looking down at myself. I was high up in the sky, and it looked the same as it had when I had floated up in the sky as a young girl. All the people had disappeared, and I could see the tops of all the buildings. Only this time someone beckoned to me to come through a door. It was so peaceful that I almost went. Then I said I would come back later if it was all right, as my children were so young." The patient learned from the nurse that her heart had stopped. She had been gasping for breath, but no one had noticed. Fortunately, the patient in the next room had a private nurse who passed by the woman's door and observed that she was in need of help.

Out-of-body experiences often appear to have no reason or purpose. There are numerous reports of floating through a door or down a hallway, of drifting over a forest or field, and of other similar journeys that seem to have no real value or use. The above story, wherein the young girl floated up high and could see no people around, seemed at the time a rather aimless excursion. However, in later life, the meaning of her earlier childhood experience crystallized when she became aware that at the time she had her second OBE she was gasping for breath in a hospital room and there were indeed no people around.

We are asked such questions as "Why did I go on an out-of-body trip to a hotel in Japan? I didn't know anyone there and couldn't understand anything being said. So what was I doing there?" The explanation will most likely come to you in the future, and no amount of impatience can produce the answer until the mind is ready to reveal it. The OBE many times is a preface to events you will experience during your entire life span. It also helps develop a creative imagination and the energy needed to achieve a goal you may wish to pursue.

In a series of interviews with professional people, it was determined that OBEs during early childhood had helped the subject decide the profession he would later choose for his life's work. For example, one man as a young boy had a toothache but was unable to see a dentist because it was Sunday. Since the pain was not severe, his mother accepted a late Monday appointment for her son. On Monday morning, the boy claimed he had an out-of-body experience and "floated over to the dentist's office, where he saw the dentist pulling a tooth." He was surprised at the simplicity of the techniques for extracting a tooth. This OBE helped to alleviate the child's fear of having a tooth pulled. Because the boy was so impressed by his "visit" during that early OBE, he decided to go into the field of dentistry. Today he is a successful dentist.

A commercial airline pilot tells us that as a young child he had a sensation of flying and seeing many places all over the world. In many OBEs as a child he did not understand why he was visiting these strange places or what relationship the trips had to anything. However, seeing a variety of countries throughout the world stimulated the child's imagination and triggered an interest in flying. As an adult, he attributed to those early OBEs the fact that he went into aviation and became a professional pilot.

These are only two of many examples in which we see the value of the OBE in determining a choice of vocation, careers in which the persons involved are happy and content. The OBE is a doorway to creativity. Once it is opened, the person sees reality in a peaceful and fearless manner. Many times he is motivated to take a new path in his life. The OBE enables a person to channel his vision and intuition into creativity.

In a parapsychology classroom students were asked to relate various experiences they felt might be psychic in nature. One member of the class, Joachim, spoke of a childhood experience he could not classify. His dog, Bo, was missing. Bo often took midnight strolls around the countryside but always returned home. However, after one such evening, the dog failed to come back. Joachim, extremely unhappy, sat in his chair and began to think about his dog. "As I did, I felt something leaving me. I looked back and saw myself on the chair, but I could hear Bo calling me. Then the part leaving me went and saw Bo, and I could see exactly where he was. He had fallen into a deep hole and couldn't get out. Suddenly, I woke up and told my father. We went to look in the place I had seen, and there we found Bo." Joachim recalled that while he was exceedingly happy about finding the dog and about having had the experience that enabled him to do so, he was somewhat apprehensive on one count. Upon "returning" to the chair, he felt his body stiff and rigid, particularly his legs, and was temporarily alarmed that something had happened to him physically because of "another part" of him being away from himself. It was explained to Joachim in class that many sensations may occur in the OBE, such as tingling, jerking, or the rigidity he experienced, but that none of them are cause for alarm. They are only temporary sensations and appear to be part of the out-of-body experience for some people. Others hear the sound of wind; still others have no sensation other than that of floating or drifting.

How can we explain to very young children what is happening in an out-of-body experience? Perhaps if we teach them *how* to experience it, they can treat it as naturally as any other educational instruction they receive. For example, a very simple lesson we call the "Fly-in Experiment" consists simply of teaching children how to "travel" under the pages of a book that is turned upside down and then tell what they "see" there. It is a very simple and uncomplicated procedure. The main thing to remember is that young children have a short attention span. Until their enthusiasm is engaged a great deal will depend upon the approach and tone of the parent or teacher who is instructing them. An encouraging word is the key to furthering a child's achievement. The OBE is something like electricity: It's always been there; it just had to be discovered.

Here is a "Fly-in" lesson for children:

1. Open a book or magazine without looking at it, and turn it over, facedown.
2. The secret now is breathing and relaxation. Tell the children to take three or four deep breaths.
3. Ask them to think of something that made them very happy.
4. Ask them to breathe and think of themselves floating. Say "Think of yourself as being light as a bird, flying through the sky to a nice white cloud."
5. Again, breathe three or four times. "You feel so light, just like a cloud. You have lost your body now and you are so light you can go anywhere you want to go."
6. "Now, in the middle of your forehead, pretend that you have an eye, a third eye. In that eye is a little ball of light. That light is the energy from your mind that is you. That is energy, the smallest ball of light you can think of, like a little pinpoint."
7. The children should be told again to relax, for the next step is extremely important: "I don't want you to worry about

what you see but only to tell me what you see. Don't try to make any associations. If you see red, just tell me you see red. If you see something round, just let me know it's round. If you see something square that is blue, just say a blue square. Unless you can clearly see what it is, don't try to guess."

8. Continue explaining to the children what they may anticipate seeing: "In the beginning you are going to start out seeing only forms and shapes and colors. Eventually, the objects themselves come into view after you practice enough, over and over again."

9. Return to the relaxation instruction: "Now let's go back and breathe softly three or four more times. Let's put that little ball of light right back into focus again like a third eye in the middle of the forehead." Breathe once or twice more and then say, "Mind, go under that book and onto those two pages and tell me what is there."

10. The person giving the test should say, "Don't take too long, just a few seconds, because you may start using your imagination. Just tell me the first thing the third eye sees." Then again say, "Mind, go back under that book and tell me a little more. What do you see? Breathe three or four more times and think of something extremely happy. Then open your eyes and come back."

To summarize, the main points to remember are:

- Open a magazine facedown without looking at it.
- Ask the child to take a few deep breaths, and then think of something happy and relaxing.
- Tell the child to breathe deeply again and imagine himself floating. In the middle of his forehead, he is to create a little ball of light.

- Tell the child "Breathe again, and once you have this energy in the light, tell the mind to go under the book and see what is there."

Children enter into the test with great enthusiasm, and we have seen some startling results.

The following examples illustrate how the OBEs of children can be helpful:

A young mother had lost her set of keys for the house, for the car, for everything. When her young daughter learned of the loss, she said to her mother, "Let me 'fly' to find them." The child claimed to have had out-of-body experiences, and the mother agreed to see if the keys could be found in this manner. The little girl sat in her rocking chair and started rocking. After a few minutes, she stopped and said to her mother, "I flew to where your keys are. Go to the garage and look into the bag of garbage you just threw out. That's where they are." The mother filtered through the garbage bag in the garage, and found the keys. Here we see that the OBE may also contain other psychic happenings, such as clairvoyance, for the child "saw" the keys while "flying." The OBE may account for many psychic experiences.

In another instance, a nine-year-old boy was home sick. He was upset because he didn't want to miss a mathematics class that day. He was poor in the subject and felt that in order to do his homework he needed the instructions that would be given in the class. The boy, by following the instructions of how to go under the magazine, tried to see if he could go to the classroom and get the material he needed. He then wrote down what he saw when he "flew" to the classroom, what examples were on the blackboard, etc. He called his mother in, gave her the paper, and asked her to deliver it to the teacher. The teacher was astounded at the accuracy of the boy's paper.

Each step of the "Fly-in" test instructions helps children reach an altered state of consciousness without having to go through long periods of meditation. Being able to achieve the OBE enables them to direct their vision and intuition creatively. When children are anxious or concerned, the OBE can also prevent them from becoming ill by enabling them to solve their problems in a constructive, creative manner.

Any psychic experience should be treated as a natural occurrence. No child should be placed on a pedestal or encouraged to perform before an audience. We encourage the out-of-body experience, not to have children think of themselves as performing magic or unusual feats or breaking any moral code but rather to show that the OBE is a part of their cycle of growth and the opening of doors to their creative ability. All psychic experiences, whether they be color experiences, dreams, imaginary playmates, or OBEs, help to develop the holistic person, thereby attuning children to their universe. Thus, his creative ability will enable him to contribute in meaningful ways to the creation of a new universe, a universe free from ills. If we examine some of the great ideas of man, we come upon such people as Edison, Einstein, and Pasteur, whose psychic sense helped them to make their discoveries. Niels Bohr, the famous atomic scientist, relates an odd experience he had as a student in college. Bohr dreamed he was on a sun made up of burning gas. Planets appeared, moving around the sun, connected by minute threads. Upon waking, he had the basis for his atomic model.

How does one distinguish an OBE from a dream? Let's turn to a historian who has had many OBE experiences since childhood:

"These strange occurrences began around the age of nine. They always occurred at night while I was asleep. All of a sudden, I would feel a shaking of my body, and I would hear a sound like the wind. I would feel myself rising out of the bed. I would go to a place just below the ceiling and would look down and see myself fast asleep in the bed. After that, I would drift through the ceiling. Sometimes I would arrive at a place which could only be described as the North Pole, all icebergs and cold. Other times, I was on the deck of a ship that had hit an iceberg and began to sink, and I would struggle from deck to deck to get above the water. I knew I had to get back to my own body in order to be saved. I would go back in an instant. Other times, I would arrive in a department store. It might be nine-thirty or ten in the morning, when it was opening.

"The experiences were never the same, but over the years I have had an infinite variety of them. For a long time, I thought they were just dreams, but even when I was young I sensed they were a 'different' kind of dream than the usual ones I had. In a regular dream, it was as though I were watching myself on television. In other words, I could see myself and all other members of the dream acting out what the dream was about. However, in these 'different' dreams, as I called them, I could never see myself floating. I could only see the part of me asleep in the bed. All I knew was that a part of me was having an experience. Many years later, after discussions with those knowledgeable of psychic matters, I learned that the nature of these experiences was out-of-body. For years I lived in anxiety about these so-called nightmares. However, now that I have learned more about them, I no longer fear them but actually look forward to the travel excursions."

In discussions with out-of-body travelers, the one thread running through all of their descriptions is that the person is convinced he views things from a position in space outside of his body, just as clearly as if he had physically been at that spot seeing it with his eyes. Another recurring theme is "You don't have the same out-of-body experience twice." They may be similar but never exactly alike. The feeling of floating and drifting—of traveling outside the body—may be a dreamlike experience. However, it generally occurs with such vivid and lifelike realism that the person experiencing it finds it difficult to accept that it is just a dream.

The out-of-body "phenomenon" is not a rarity but almost a commonplace occurrence. Each of us may know of someone who has had at least one out-of-body experience. The very fact that these experiences can be found within one's own circle of friends or family makes it easier to accept that they do happen and to real people, not to magicians or fakes. Being aware of this freedom of thought, we can now give freedom to the mind—to our children's as well as our own—in our bodies or out of them!

Part Two

Stages of

Development

Six

The Child from Conception to the Sixth Year

While it is generally accepted that parents will have an effect upon their child's personality and future life after he or she is born, we support the new theory that parents start influencing their child from the time of conception.

Upon conception, a child begins to have life and consciousness. While still in the womb, a child is able to receive vibrations from the emotions of its mother and father that will affect its totality. These vibrations continue until birth.

There are many arguments as to when the fetus first is affected by outside vibrations. It is not our intent to contest any of them. The subject we are dealing with here is not so much *when* a child starts to receive these vibrations but *where* a child begins to receive them—in the womb!

A mother of two says that she knew intuitively that her first child would be a girl. She began to read to her child while it was still in the womb. She sent it thoughts of comfort and concern and kept telling it to develop reading ability. Later, a girl was born. When the girl became mature enough to read, she had an avid interest in books. She now works as an editor for a magazine.

The mother of that girl had another psychic impression while carrying her second child. This time she felt it would be a boy and sent vibrations and thoughts indicating that she wanted him to be a strong man able to excel in sports and to live a healthy life. The boy was born shortly after, and as he grew he began to excel in sports and eventually became captain of his baseball team.

The gender of a child has no bearing on the vibrations he or she receives. What is important here is that the child in the womb can receive a parent's telepathic thoughts and encouraging vibrations and that these thoughts can play a vital role in the child's future.

While we, the authors, were each in our mother's womb, our parents sent caring and encouraging thoughts to us. Katherine's mother tells of singing to her, hoping her child would be happy and able to sing. She also tells how she would write poems of happiness in her mind and think of her child as being able to write well. At an early age Katherine displayed musical ability and as a child sang on the stage, winning many contests, and later on radio programs. In high school and college, she became news editor, and later, by becoming an editor and author, she fulfilled her mother's hopes that her daughter would write.

Alex's mother began to send thoughts of love and encouragement from the time she was carrying him, talking to him of lofty ideals, urging him to overcome obstacles and to become successful in his endeavors. Alex and his seven brothers were all successful in their chosen fields before they were twenty-five. Receiving their mother's telepathic encouragement helped provide the insight required later in life to succeed.

Parents' display of negative emotions while the child is still in the womb can have a detrimental effect. The child may be unwanted, or the parents may not be ready for the responsibility of a child. Such negative emotional vibrations can have serious repercussions. We are not telling parents to be saints, but we are saying that they carry a tremendous responsibility—the life of another human being. Just as parents must care for the mother's physical condition during pregnancy to assure the physical well-being of their child, so should they care for her psychological and emotional condition. Parents should try to feel as cheerful and as positive as possible while the mother is carrying her unborn child. *The child's feeling of security or insecurity may well be established at that time.*

Up to the age of two or so, a child gathers more and more understanding from the vibrations of his parents. When parents speak to a child, he receives what is being said both verbally and telepathically. The child may not be able to understand the language, but he can understand the intonation. Furthermore, a child can sense whether his mother has positive or negative thoughts toward him, even though she may attempt to disguise them. Experts assert that the most important relationship a child has before the age of two is with his mother. Dr. Jan Ehrenwald describes the telepathic relationship between the very young baby and his mother thus:

> The mother-child relationship has always been considered a source of profound emotional closeness and communicative intimacy between the two. Whether or not a telepathic element is involved in this state of affairs is still a matter of controversy. The problem is thrown into sharper perspective, however, when we turn our attention to the early symbiotic relationship between mother and child—where "it all started" in the first place. . . .
>
> The baby is a direct extension of his mother's body image. She "does the doing" for him. She feeds him when he is hungry. She gives him warmth when he is cold. She lifts his covers

when he is warm. She diapers him when he is wet. She monitors his physical and social environment on his behalf. She is the omnipotent, omniscient, bountiful mother figure.[1]

Dr. Ehrenwald explains that these are merely "descriptive terms" that have little relation to the reality and that

it is at this point that the telepathy hypothesis comes to our rescue. . . .

Telepathy, to the extent that it is taken for granted by the general public, is usually considered as a mere psychological curiosity; as a freakish and ambiguous means of communication, without an apparent goal or discernible purpose. Conversely, we have seen that the early symbiotic phase confronts us with a relative communication gap in the mother-child dual [sic] without a tangible means to bridge it. The fact is that in the preverbal or nonverbal phase signals are exchanged and mutual cueing occurs in a way which runs far ahead of the infant's capacity to make himself understood. At the same time mother seems to "understand" in a way which is difficult to account for in terms of the "ordinary" means of communication.

Thus, introducing the telepathy hypothesis into the . . . parent-child relationship helps to fill the gap in our understanding of its functioning. But it does more than that; it assigns an important physiological function to an otherwise seemingly superfluous vehicle of communication, to telepathy. It accounts for the modus operandi of the exchange of an infinite variety of primitive or proto-messages, preverbal instructions and injunctions between mother and child. At the same time, it suggests that telepathy is in effect the embryological matrix of communication which is later destined to be superseded by speech. . . .

To be more precise . . . telepathy follows the pattern of intra-psychic communication within one single, psychologically as yet undifferentiated personality structure.[2]

That telepathy is indeed an important means of communication is also borne out by the following telepathic communication between *father* and child.

A two-year-old boy was sitting with his parents on a couch. The child was looking at a cartoon on television when suddenly he jumped up and turned the TV station to a sports game. There was no verbal communication, but—at the very moment the child changed the station—the father was thinking how he would prefer seeing the baseball game. The child picked up his father's thought and switched the channel. Telepathy seems to be a strong psychic link between parent and child at this age level.

Between the ages of two and five, children begin to use language in sentence form. During this period they can talk about psychic experiences they have been having. They may speak of strange dreams, imaginary playmates, or "floating" out of their bodies. Children begin to have telepathic and precognitive experiences that they can convey verbally. Parents should be attentive and understanding, because it is now that the development of a child's psychic abilities begins.

We just saw how a two-year-old boy acted upon nonverbal communication of a psychic impression. Now let's look at the case of a boy of six who was able to verbally relate a psychic impression he received of impending danger. He rushed up to his teacher, crying out, "I want to go home. I want to go home!" The teacher asked why. "The furnace is bad. It's going to blow up. My sister is home and she can burn up." The teacher didn't know what to do. She thought the boy had gone crazy or was having an attack of some kind. She called his parents at work and discovered that the boy's sister was indeed home that day with a bad cold. His father came to pick the boy up, and the mother went directly home, where she found the furnace so high that it was ready to explode. She was just in time. When the child's father came to the school to get him, he suddenly quieted down and said, "We don't have to go home now. Mama is home and everything's okay." The boy's words were spoken after his mother had turned off the furnace.

Because the parents heeded the psychic impression of their young son, they saved their daughter's life. While parents cannot allow their lives to be ruled by a child's prognostications, it is important for them to pay attention to their content. Even if a so-called prediction does not come true parents should not scoff but should sympathize with what their child is experiencing.

The period from two to six is the critical time in the development of a child's personality. Four basic problem types surface more than others: choleric, sanguine, melancholic, and phlegmatic.

The *choleric* child is rapidly and vehemently agitated by outside impressions. He or she reacts spontaneously, and the impressions and agitation last a long time. In fact they generally induce further excitement in the child—a self-propelling type of thing. The choleric child feels deeply hurt if humiliated or shamed by parents or peers. His anger is immediate and long-lasting. He reacts violently to contradictions, resistance, and what he considers personal offenses. This personality generally considers reproaches to be both false and highly exaggerated. When the choleric indulges himself in furious outbursts of anger, his anger very quickly generates into hatred. He dislikes others and is often deceitful.

On the brighter side, a choleric child aspires to the noble and heroic, looking down on vulgarity. He or she usually displays a keen intellect and a strong will. There is an avid passion to rule or to be in a position of command. The choleric child has a natural bent for organizing other children in play and games.

In working with cholerics, parents and teachers should never allow themselves to display extreme anger. Furthermore, they should never express a desire to "break" the choleric child. It is very important that parents and teachers remain calm and allow the child to "cool off." This can sometimes be accomplished by a period of meditation, after which the child should be persuaded to accept help in correcting his faults and bringing out the good in him. It is particularly important for the choleric child that his parents place high ideals before him and appeal to his goodwill and sense of honor.

When the need arises to punish a choleric child, try to show him the necessity and the justice of the punishment without inflicting humiliation. For example, if a choleric child throws a temper tantrum at the table, a parent should take the child to his room and tell him he will have to stay there until he calms down. It should be explained that it is not fair to force the rest of the family to eat during a tantrum. The child should be told that if he has a complaint, he can voice it before or after dinner but not in a disruptive fashion. Under no circumstances should a choleric child be beaten. He will not respond to physical punishment; on the contrary, his anger will build to unscalable peaks. When the ideals of the choleric child are appealed to, he may respond in a more positive manner. If he is permitted to maintain his pride, giant strides can be made.

The *sanguine* child's anger is also aroused quickly, but it is very short-lived. The sanguine child can change his mood quickly. He is generally erratic in his opinions. Before he has absorbed one subject, his interest flits to another area, especially if it does not require deep thought or great effort. Two of the main traits of the sanguine child are his superficial evaluation of situations and his instability. Other points recognizable in the sanguine child may be extreme vanity, jealousy, or envy. In their amusements, such children are often very frivolous. The sanguine child wants to enjoy life but just can't decide what it will take to provide that enjoyment.

Positive points of the sanguine child include the ability to make friends easily with other children. He is very pleasant and generally willing to oblige. The sanguine child is compassionate if one of his friends is hurt. Although this temperament leads the child to be quickly excited by the slightest offense, he gives vent to his wrath very fast, gets over it, and is pleasant again in short order. He carries no grudge. On the whole, the sanguine child is both pliable and docile. While most children find it hard to be obedient, the sanguine child does not.

It is important for the parents and teachers of this child to realize that his words should not be taken too seriously. His resolutions and promises are generally very short-lived. He must be constantly checked on as to whether he has done his home tasks and studies. It is important to teach him perseverance and observation of order. The sanguine child must be kept under constant supervision and guidance. This is particularly true in order to guard him against the behavior of bad companions, because he can be easily swayed and taken in by others with questionable motives. Because he is naturally cheerful and fun-loving, his parents have to watch that he does not go overboard in pursuing his pleasures.

Another important point is that the sanguine child is a "tattle-tale." His parents must train him to be circumspect in his speech, since he will have a strong tendency to tell tales out of school. He must be taught why it is important to keep certain information in confidence.

The *melancholic* child shows little reaction to any outside disturbances. Either the reaction never sets in or it does so only after a long period of time. However, when those impressions are repeated and do indeed set into the melancholic child's mind, they remain deeply rooted. If subsequent outside disturbances continue over a period of time, they fill the child's mind to such a degree that only with difficulty can they be eradicated. The fundamental disposition of the melancholic child is one of passivity and self-reflection. The melancholic is generally overly serious about actions around him, even to the point of being morbid. Because he is inclined to introspection, he withdraws from crowds and people and has strong desires to be alone. He is slow in speech and often stutters or leaves his sentences incomplete. The melancholic child may move and walk in an awkward manner. A telling trait is that a melancholic child rarely forgives offenses against him. While he may not react to the first, second, or even third offense, he will eventually resent a continued pattern of misbehavior and will hold a permanent grudge against the offender.

Since the melancholic child takes life so seriously, and is inclined to self-reflection, he often develops into a deep thinker and philosopher. In later life, he may follow a religious calling, become a social worker, or take on a career as an artist, writer, or poet. Generally, he is a good counselor in difficulties, because he is prudent and trustworthy. On the whole, he has a desire to help humanity.

Teachers should take extra care to be kind and friendly to melancholic children, who must be taught to pronounce words properly and to use all of their senses to observe the exterior world. Because melancholics take everything to heart and are extremely sensitive, any necessary punishment must be limited. The slightest appearance of harshness should be avoided. While not overburdening these children with work, parents and teachers should try to keep them busy so they does not withdraw to an inner world. The most important advice we can give parents is to have patience with the child's slow actions and try to get him to exercise in as vigorous a manner as he can. Swimming would be a very good way to start in this direction and would help resolve the problem of his awkward movement.

The mind of the *phlegmatic* child is rarely touched by outside impressions. If there is a reaction, it is very feeble, and such impressions quickly disappear. Unfortunately the phlegmatic child has little interest in what is going on around him. He has little inclination to work and an inordinate desire for leisure.

On the positive side, the phlegmatic child may work slowly, but he perseveres if the work does not require too much thinking. He is rarely troubled by failures or so-called offenses. While many children will back away from anything smacking of failure, the phlegmatic child is not interested in success or failure but rather in persevering in the work he is told to do. Generally, such a child is thoughtful and deliberate, having sober and practical judgment.

The education of phlegmatic children is very difficult, for external influences have little effect upon them. It is necessary to train them through constant repetition so that some impression may be made to last.

In describing the four main personality groups, we have attempted to advise parents and teachers on how to teach these children in a normal way at home and at school, along with their siblings in the home and their playmates in the classroom. We believe that *all* children, including those with personality problems, have psychic abilities.

The child's psychic ability can lessen his negative qualities and increase his positive ones. The development of a child's psychic awareness can lead him along a creative path to where he can adjust his personality to his environment.

When a choleric child has one of his fierce temper tantrums, he also has spontaneous psychic experiences. The wild emotion sets off something in the mind that opens it to psychic phenomena and seems to speed up the triggering of the experience. It is important to remember that when this violence erupts and opens up the mind to psychism, the experience is generally short-lived. The parents must pick it up immediately because the child does not remember what he said. In our experience, the most common psychic experience that comes through at such times is precognition. Many parents of choleric children have said that when their child is in this state he or she seems "possessed." This is not the case. It is merely a reaction of the choleric personality to the triggering of the psychic force and has nothing to do with the demonic. In the Bible there are many examples testifying that when an epileptic is going into a fit are able to foresee the future and to prophesy. Generally, a choleric child has strong psychic ability that can be used to help change him from a "temper-tantrum thrower" to a "calm, collected child."

Meditation is one of the most important quieting steps for a choleric child. The meditation should be approached as a game and can consist of discussing pleasant times he has experienced and stories aimed at getting him to relax. The calming effect is a preparatory step to taking ESP tests. In the meditative story, a parent or teacher might incorporate the fact that Jack the Rabbit was doing ESP tests, cutting cards, looking at symbols, etc., and that "we are going to do this very shortly." In this way the child can be calmed down and prepared for the tests simultaneously.

In our research, we have observed that the length of a child's anger is gradually shortened through the use of these methods. If a child has a fit that lasts twenty to twenty-five minutes, through meditation and ESP testing the period can generally be reduced to four or five minutes. At her wits' end with her choleric son's outbursts, a mother who had been attending a parapsychology class came to one of us for advice. She wanted to know how his psychic abilities could be directed to help alleviate the tension he was causing at home and in the classroom. She was told to have her child spend approximately twenty-five minutes each day meditating. Afterward, she was to conduct ESP tests with the child for about ten minutes. She was cautioned not to expect miraculous results overnight. After three years of patience and perseverance, the woman reported very good progress. Her son is no longer considered "the menace" of his classroom.

The sanguine child is easier to work with, because his temper outbursts are much shorter. Furthermore, the sanguine child does not harbor the hatred of the choleric. If another child punches him, the choleric child will bite, scream, kick, and probably hate that child for the rest of his life. The sanguine child will forget it, especially if the experience occurs only once or twice. On the other hand, the sanguine child is deeply affected by a repetition of the same experience.

The sanguine child requires less meditation than the choleric child. The ideal period of meditation is around fifteen minutes. On the other hand, the sanguine child should be tested for his psychic abilities for a somewhat longer period, for approximately thirty minutes after the meditation period. Remember that the sanguine personality loves diversity and that constant repetition is boring to him. Therefore, the ESP tests should be rotated.

Among the negative attitudes of the phlegmatic child are his constant introspection and his long periods of silence and withdrawal. Parents and teachers must be aware that with this type of temperament the meditation period must be short. Since the phlegmatic child prefers the pursuit of pleasure to anything else, both the meditation period and the ESP tests must be geared along pleasure lines. For example, during a meditation period of four or five minutes the child should be led to think about pleasant experiences in his life. If he finds this difficult to do, the adult should relate a pleasurable experience from his or her own childhood. Repetition is important in the teaching of a phlegmatic child. So it is with the ESP tests. First, the test must be simple. The same test should be repeated until the child shows a psychic response above chance. The best test for the phlegmatic child is conducted with an ordinary deck of playing cards. The tester picks a jack out of the deck and shows it to the child, then replaces it and shuffles the cards. He then tells the child to think about that card and pick it out of the deck by cutting the deck of cards. Testing the phlegmatic child is a long process, but with patience and understanding the negative part of his nature weakens while his positive points slowly help him develop a holistic personality.

The phlegmatic child has spurts of creative activity. He may express this by drawing with color crayons or building with blocks. Unfortunately these spurts are generally only brief, whereupon the child reverts to the introspection he prefers. In 1974, after a lecture dealing with how to use a child's psychic abilities to help him develop into a holistic person, a father told the speaker about problems he was having with his son. The speaker presents his ideas of testing children for their psychic abilities and asked the father if his son liked to do things with his hands. The father acknowledged that he did, but rarely. "He seems to be able to put blocks together and build little houses and bridges and things like that." The speaker then told the father that he should start the child on an extensive period of testing with a deck of cards, repeating a simple test over and over again. He also suggested that the father buy his son a set of Lincoln logs and display it during the ESP tests. For four years, the father persevered in testing his son with the toys and cards. In the spring of 1978, during another lecture series in Georgia, the father came up with his son, who said to the speaker, "You are the man who got me to play with my toys again." The father told the speaker that not only was his son playing with the Lincoln logs and square blocks, but the year before he had asked for an erector set and built four or five projects in the basement. The child is in school, and although he still has periods of "relaxation" from his creative abilities, they are becoming less and less pronounced.

Methods of working with melancholic children should be somewhat similar to those of working with phlegmatics, for both are slow to respond to outside forces. Both can harbor a sense of frustration and withdrawal for a long time. Therefore, the tests given to the melancholic child should be similar to those given to the phlegmatic but with a different approach. The meditation period should be no longer than four or five minutes. Since the melancholic child is so overwhelmingly concerned with himself, he should be told to think of a pleasant experience that one of his friends has had rather than he himself. Thus we try to bring him out of his shell and to think about the environment and those around him. The ESP tests should begin in a simple but can be rapidly upgraded to more sophisticated types. Tests given to a melancholic should be rotated constantly. Since this child is given to depression and introspection, and we want to bring him out of himself, it is good to let him act as tester with another child, allowing the ESP testing to help get the melancholic child to think about people other than himself.

Let's remember that our aim here is to make the child holistic and to direct creativity into positive channels for his future development and achievement. A healthy body is a healthy mind. A healthy mind is a healthy body. Perhaps advice to parents and teachers can best be summarized as: "The fruit of the spirit is love, joy, peace, patience, kindness, goodness, faithfulness, gentleness and self-control" (Galatians 5:22–23).

Seven

Educating the Two Sides of the Brain

The fact that the human brain is divided into two parts—one responsible for logic and analytical thought, and the other responsible for intuitive and spatial understanding—is well documented in scientific literature, but what is not as recognized and understood is the implications they might have in the field of child education. We firmly believe there is an important need for the education of both sides of the brain and that the best way to do this is through understanding and developing children's intuitive abilities—their psychic awareness.

Educational programs restricted to reading, writing, and arithmetic serve to educate only one side of the brain, ignoring the potential of the intuitive side. Supporting this theory is neurosurgeon Dr. J. E. Bogen, who states that such an educational program "will educate mainly one hemisphere, leaving half of an individual's high-level potential unschooled."[1]

Dr. Bogen indicates that people whose only education consists of the three Rs may suffer underdevelopment, and similarly that capacities of the right hemisphere can suffer neglect. There is a real need to promote both approaches to knowledge—through both the logical and the intuitive sides of the brain—in public education, in research, and in the everyday life of the child at home.

Dr. Paul F. Brandwein, another innovator in the study of the differences between the left and right sides of the brain, is the author of *The Teaching of Science* and *The Permanent Agenda of Man.* Dr. Brandwein is a member of the National Humanities Faculty, adjunct professor at the University of Pittsburgh, and a former senior vice president and director of Harcourt Brace Jovanovich, where he headed the school curriculum and instruction group. An early experimenter in nongraded instruction. Dr. Brandwein has devoted much time to consulting with school systems on curricula and teaching. He has taught at all levels of instruction—elementary, secondary, undergraduate, and graduate—and is now interested in developing a total, coordinated elementary-school curriculum. A part of this concept-seeking is the duality of the mind, about which Dr. Brandwein has this to say:

Because time is short, both in a person's lifetime and in the period of his schooling, we may ask which concepts are worth the time that is given over to schooling. Surely language is essential. Are not science and mathematics vitally important in our modern technology? Yet do we then need only scientists and engineers in our society? To ask the question is to pose the answer: No. Even a casual glance at a day in the life of *Homo faber* (technological man and woman) shows how much we depend on music, art, dance, drama, and graphic experience—whether TV, theater, museums, or libraries. Hobby or avocation is important—almost as important as the job. We recognize that hobbies are a way in which we, consciously but not harmfully, gain relief from our professional and perhaps even civic responsibilities. Does this mean that science, mathematics, and logic are the main users of the mind, and that, conversely, esthetics are a lesser use? Is art a "relief" taken from more serious pursuits? Recent researches on the function of the brain may clarify our reflection on these matters.

It is becoming ever clearer that the right and left brains have specialized functions. In the main, the left brain seems specialized in the *verbal-linear* modes. In research on split-brain, right-handed individuals it seems to be the repository for language and mathematics. The right brain is specialized in the *spatio-visual holistic* modes, and it would seem to function strongly in painting, sculpture, dance, and other skills that depend on nonverbal cognition.[2]

Brandwein holds that music, art, and dance

employ associative, nonlinear patterns that have great appeal. The right brain responds to rhythm, combinations of sounds, and assortments of shapes and colors prompting spontaneous expression. The child proceeds naturally and freely as he engages in these activities.

Intuition should be considered as a complementary function of intelligence. Partially, the strength of the individual comes from intelligence, but coupled with this is intuition, which I call a leap in the dark, a little recognized quality which needs mothering and fathering.

Intuition has no limitations imposed by structure. For example you manage your classroom, evaluate student progress, and diagnose problems—to a great extent—intuitively. You often know when a student is having a problem before it surfaces.

Children are bombarded with "How did you get the answer?" "How did you decide on that?" "How did you figure the problem?" Sometimes they look vague or embarrassed because they are unable to respond or unwilling to admit that the solution came partially from intuitive thinking.[3]

While a good portion of the above material is directed to teachers, it can also aid parents in their efforts to help children understand the ways knowledge can be acquired and to apply their knowledge in useful and constructive ways. Some children find it much easier to solve problems using verbal symbols than visual-spatial ones. Michael S. Gazzaniga (in "Review of the Split Brain," UCLA *Educator*) talks of problems, discouragement, and possible hostility that might be avoided by permitting a child to use his special talents:

> When a child's talents lie in visual-spatial relations and (s)he is being forced into a curriculum that emphasizes the verbal articulatory modes of solving a conceptual problem, this child will encounter enormous frustration and difficulty which may well result in hostility toward the teacher and worse, toward the learning process itself. If the teacher were to be made aware that the child is specialized in visual-spatial skills and the same conceptual problem is introduced, both the discouragement and the subsequent hostility might be avoided if the child is allowed to use his special talents. Conversely, the child with high verbal skills may quite frequently be unable to visualize the spatial aspect of an assigned task; in this case also, far better results could be obtained if (s)he is not forced into academic areas for which (s)he is not naturally equipped.[4]

Returning for a moment to Dr. Bogen, an enormously important question then arises: "Is the IQ a measure only of the left brain? Does it measure but 'one-half' our potential"? Bogen's question might be further posed: Is a reevaluation of the effectiveness of present learning processes in the schools needed? Are we penalizing children who could be progressing through proper education of the intuitive process?

For the past fifty years there has been a growing tendency to educate the young for the advancement of technology and science. We have pushed our children into becoming engineers, doctors, scientists, computer specialists, and businesspeople. The educational system has been geared to the maximum use of the logical side of man. However, we feel that the time has now arrived for a child's creative ability, the intuitive side of his or her brain, to be given equal time.

Mankind's advances in technology and science have so far outstripped his humanistic tendencies that we are in danger of obliterating ourselves. What humanity needs in order to catch up with its own technology is to allow the right, intuitive side of the brain to flower. We have been suffering from the so-called "cultural lag" wherein man has built weapons that can destroy himself without knowing how to control them. *Perhaps through the balancing of intuition with logic our next generation can establish a balance between man's humanity and his inhumanity!*

Eight

Psychic Development
of the Child

Telepathy, clairvoyance, precognition, and the whole spectrum of psychic experiences have played an important role in the lives of many creative individuals of note: author and lecturer Mark Twain, inventor Thomas Edison, poet and dramatist Johann Goethe, composer and musician Robert Schumann, novelist Ernest Hemingway, mathematician and scientist Albert Einstein, author Graham Greene, and countless others. In fact, so many ESP experiences were reported by highly creative persons that an entire volume on them, *Noted Witnesses for Psychic Occurrences*,[1] was published.

How can these talents be developed and utilized to further a child's creativity? Rather than look to the child, we must first examine the attitude of parents and teachers. In recent correspondence, Mrs. Eloise Shields, a psychologist with the California school system, enlightened us about some adult reactions to one child's psychic experiences:

In children who are telepathic, I have found that adults often react with fear or withdrawal, on the supposition that "if he can read my mind in this one thing, he can read my mind on every area of my unconscious," which is rather fearsome. Adults tend to become threatened, not realizing that what the child telepathizes is only a mere bit of data, not "everything." All people have stored bits in the unconscious which are kept private and not known to anyone else, and the adults (parents and teachers, at least) seem to be afraid that the child will bring out some of this *verboten* material. It is rare that this happens, but I have seen parents and teachers who avoided or withdrew from telepathic children because of this.

With teachers who have had a child telepathize something in the classroom, they are put into a more "human" role than just a teacher. They are also a person. This is a subtle relationship change which some teachers like, but others cannot cope with except [by] withdrawing from the child emotionally so as not to let this happen.

Other teachers are quite intrigued by this phenomenon, or with clairvoyance, precognition and other psi events. They encourage children in their classrooms to report it. This is especially true, I've found, with teachers of retarded children, who are delighted to realize that the child has potential that they hadn't realized. They often will encourage more of this, which the child then verbalizes.

If a child who has exhibited psychic ability is in either a negative or fearful environment, he or she will be kept back from true creative development. How should a child's ESP be handled? Some parents or teachers may ignore or ridicule a child's experiences, whereas others may want to "show off" the child to family and friends as a "psychic whiz kid." Either extreme can be detrimental. The most helpful thing parents and teachers can do is to give relaxed encouragement, letting things happen in a natural way. The child should not be coaxed or pressured to give demonstrations on demand. Psychic experiences are spontaneous, and pushing a child to produce them may diminish the very things parents and teachers wish to encourage. Some of the things parents may wish to do to help in a positive manner are:

- Create an atmosphere of understanding and caring so that the child will not be afraid to tell you of his experiences.
- Give older children books on ESP or read portions to the younger ones. (Some suggestions appear in "Suggested Reading.")
- Keep a record of psychic happenings in order to see if there are any trends.
- Respond to whatever experience the child relates to you in a natural way: "Isn't that interesting" or "Oh, you picked up my thought." Encourage the child to talk about his dreams or any other experiences.
- Give ESP tests, treating them in a gamelike fashion, with both parents and children participating, or encourage the child to play guessing games of a similar nature with friends.

It is up to parents and teachers to foster an atmosphere that will enable the child to use his psychic ability in his creative work, be it studies, art, music, play, sports, or what have you, for, as the noted Dr. Gardner Murphy states, "There actually *is* a relation between creativeness and extrasensory perception."[2]

Everyone, child or adult, has either had or heard of psychic experiences at some time or another. If a child wishes to tell his parents about a psychic experience, they should accept the fact that something has happened—whether they call it coincidence or otherwise—and that their child is looking to them for some explanation. If the parents receive his or her statements in a negative manner, the child may never approaches them again. In suffering rebuke or disappointment, two very important things may take place: the child and parent may lose the initial faith and trust that can be established by being able to talk about problem areas such as an unusual dream, and, as a consequence, the child may suppress ideas. In the first instance, great hostility may result on the part of the child toward the parent; in the second, the child's inventiveness and creativity may be greatly diminished if not lost.

What happened to one pregnant mother is an example of how a positive response, rather than a negative one, helped her child. The woman's nine-year-old daughter came to her in the early part of June and told her she would have a baby boy whose weight would be a little over six pounds. She said, too, that the boy would be born on June 14. The woman replied, "How interesting. How do you know?" "I just saw it, that's all," said her child. On June 14, the woman gave birth to a baby boy weighing six pounds, four ounces.

Had there been a negative response from the mother, her daughter might have become frightened or inhibited. The mother, too, if suffering from the misconception that psychic experiences are to be feared, could have had an adverse reaction during her pregnancy or the delivery of the child. The very fact that the mother did not reject her young daughter's precognitive statement led to the child's feeling of acceptance when the new baby arrived. Moreover, the young daughter felt a "part of things," because she had made the prediction and was in her own way "responsible" for the baby. The child won't be afraid of her psychic ability in the future.

In another instance, a young girl was participating in a science project in school. Since her mother was taking a course in ESP and the daughter found it interesting, she decided to illustrate a test for telepathy with another classmate as her project. In the classroom, when called upon by her teacher, she and her friend sat at opposite ends of the room. The girl drew a picture on a piece of paper, and the friend at the other end of the room picked it up by telepathy and drew the same picture. The other students accused the girls of setting it up before class. The teacher, who was also skeptical, offered to participate in the experiment with the girl. The girl drew a picture of water and a nearby tree, and the teacher picked it up telepathically: His picture also contained water and a tree.

The fact that the teacher was willing to help the girl conduct her experiment, even though he was skeptical, showed that he maintained an open mind. This encouraged not only the child but also the entire class to seek more information. It opened the lines of communication in an area where the teacher had once been a nonbeliever, as were the scoffing students. The end result was that future tests were conducted in the classroom, and the girl got an A in the subject.

We have received many letters from high school students throughout the country stating that they are doing special class projects on ESP. More and more teachers and parents are accepting the idea of ESP in their children and allowing them to do research in the field. They appear to be following the advice of Dr. Gardner Murphy, who wrote in 1969: "I think that college age is the wrong age for good ESP subjects. I think that one does better in early adolescence than late. I don't know why we don't do more with high school students. I don't know why we don't do more with elementary school students."[3]

In developing the psychic abilities of a child, parents should feel and also make their child feel that this is a subject they can comfortably discuss with each other.

Many parents would like to try to make their children psychic simply because they themselves have had one or two psychic experiences. Others want to put their child on a stagelike pedestal. On the other hand, there are parents who will hide these experiences from their children or from society because they do not wish to be thought of as odd or different. *Attitude* is all important. *Comprehension* is all important.

A child should be able to transfer psychic abilities into everyday living, at school, at play, or wherever, for it is important that he be able to function successfully in his endeavors. A psychic phenomenon is the vision and the insight, and all the psychic experiences—telepathy, clairvoyance, precognition—will give the child a total picture of how to succeed.

A boy of ten was doing poorly in school, particularly with mathematics, in which he was failing. One night he had a vivid dream, in color, in which he was shown the solution to the principles of mathematics. Upon awakening, he got up, went to his mathematics book, and did all the problems. When he turned his homework in, every problem was correct. The boy is now twenty-one and is majoring in mathematics, with plans to become an electrical engineer. This is certainly a case in which psychic ability not only helped a child resolve his problem, but also became a determining factor in the selection of his future career.

It is our belief that early development of psychic abilities will help a child focus on an area of endeavor best suited to his or her abilities. In discovering his or her goal early, a child can aim toward it without having to search around, asking "What am I going to do in life?"

Parents can start determining their child's psychic ability by testing him or her with cards at the age of two. The testing, which should be conducted like a game rather than a serious business, should be an ongoing project for many years. The parents should tally the results of tests and keep them. If such testing is done on a periodic basis, the results should show the gradual growth of a child's psychic and creative ability. Scores should get higher, and the child's creativity should expand. In the following letter from John Sanbonmatsu, reprinted by permission of John and the American Society for Psychical Research, to whom the letter was directed, we see the results of an enterprising older child with his younger sister:

Enclosed are the results of an experiment which I conducted on October 31, 1976, dealing with conventional ESP. I am a

Fellow Member of the ASPR. I conducted this test completely on my own. I am fourteen years of age and I am continually experimenting with psychic phenomena and their comparison with psychology.

This test consisted of: (1) a young subject (my eleven-year-old sister), (2) five drawn targets, and (3) a small envelope with two small pieces of cardboard. The process was a simple one. I, as the experimenter, put the target inside the envelope with the pieces of cardboard on either side of it. I then sealed the envelope with a paper clip and led the subject into my room, giving her the response sheet.

When she was finished, she left the room while I prepared another target. While the subject worked on her response I watched her carefully to assure no cheating.

The reason I have sent in this letter is for your research. Although psychic phenomena themselves are not unusual, I was wondering if ESP was frequent among children (as in my subject). I enclose my diagrams and the responses.[4] [*Reprinted through the courtesy of the* ASPR Newsletter, *4 July 1977*)]

Young John is not alone in sharing such tests with a member of the family. In the material below we see the continuing creativity of the novelist Upton Sinclair, who shows that adults too are interested in participating in ESP tests. Author of more than one hundred books, Sinclair became interested in psychic matters and wrote a book about ESP experiments, *Mental Radio*.[5] The experiments consisted of Sinclair or someone else drawing a secret picture and asking his wife to draw another picture to match it. Some of the targets and responses are on the following pages.

In the last part of Figure 3, the target is the American flag, whose response could hardly be called a coincidence. It should also be noted here that sometimes the pictures were made as far apart as forty miles.

Figure 1

Many books on psychic matters have since referred to the *Mental Radio* experiments. However, probably the best comment in summing up this work was that of Professor R. A. McConnell, who states:

> One important feature of Sinclair's book is that you do not have to be a scientist to understand it. Even though you may not have studied statistics and psychology, you can read the book yourself and make up your mind as to its value on the basis of common sense. When you do, I think you will arrive at the conclusion that many scientists have reached by entirely different kinds of experiments. I think you will decide that extrasensory perception is a reality regardless of the skepticism of the psychological profession.[6]

Before proceeding to parents' testing of their children's psychic abilities, we should like to talk about an important factor in creating an atmosphere conducive to testing: meditation. For some reason, the moment the word *meditation* is mentioned, many people react with fear or withdrawal. Some worry that it deals with hypnotism or mysticism; others feel it involves some sort of prayer. These misconceptions come from the same place all misinformation comes from: the minds of those frightened by anything done in a way "different" from what is considered "normal" by society.

Meditation is exactly what it says: In meditation one meditates. How does meditation work with children and on what do they "meditate"? The parent or teacher may begin by reading a pleasant story to them or by telling them about a pleasant experience. Meditation is simply a turning inward to find a certain amount of peace and tranquility so that the creativity of the child may emerge.

There are many books relating to the development of meditation and some relating specifically to children. Formal meditation

TARGET **RESPONSE**

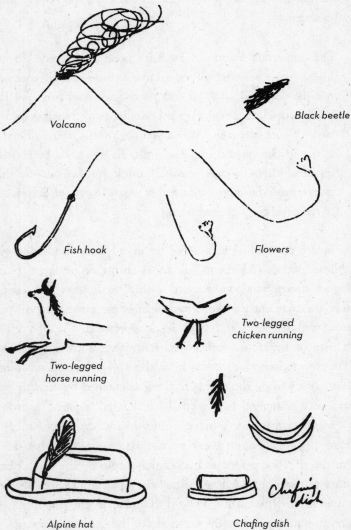

Volcano

Black beetle

Fish hook

Flowers

Two-legged
horse running

Two-legged
chicken running

Alpine hat

Chafing dish

Figure 2

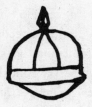

TARGET
RESPONSE
Helmet
Same idea
Target idea
Response
Stars
Stars and moon
American Flag
Response

Figure 3

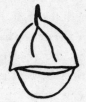

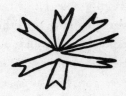

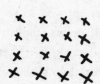

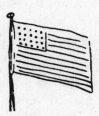

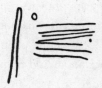

is not necessary, because the purpose here is to foster creativity, not to provide a rigid framework that will inhibit the child from expressing himself in the work we are trying to help him accomplish. On the other hand, we are not opposed to certain techniques that are now being utilized. If something doesn't work, don't push it beyond the child's capabilities. Try something else; otherwise it may hinder the child's development. *The period of meditation should come as naturally to a child as his or her afternoon nap.*

The child should be free to choose whatever position he finds most comfortable. He is then told to relax, "for we are going to try something new, something called meditation." Children generally respond to new and interesting ideas. The child may ask, "Do I have to close my eyes?" It should be left up to him; he may do whatever puts him at ease. Whatever question is asked of you— whether to sit in a certain position, close the eyes, etc.—leave the decision to the child.

Young children have a great deal of energy that has to be localized and disciplined, and meditation has proven to be an excellent way to do just that. What you wish to accomplish here is a quieting period that enables the child to relax. It is through this relaxation, rather than through concentration, that some of the best results in psychic phenomena are achieved. In concentration the child may try too hard and lose contact with reality by wondering if he is doing right or by trying to focus, thus losing the necessary spontaneity.

In a group, the parent or teacher should exercise judgment as to how long a child should meditate. In the beginning, the meditation period should be no longer than five minutes.

We suggest three kinds of meditation: musical, verbal, and the personal thought the child is called upon to evoke without the aid of music or speech.

Musical meditation consists of playing very soft, calming music.

Any of the classics or other pleasant music to meditate by may be played, although songs whose words the child knows should be avoided. The child is then asked to think of pictures that the music brings to mind. At the end of the meditation, there can be a brief discussion of the pictures he saw.

In verbal meditation the parent or teacher reads a short poem or, for younger children, a short fairy tale that is conducive to meditating. At the end of the reading, the child should be relaxed and ready to do psychic tests or to play or do other things.

In silent meditation the child is left to his own devices and told to relax and think of some pleasant experience he has had or something pleasant he would like to do and to evoke images in his mind about this activity.

During the meditation period there should be no speaking or interruptions until the period is over.

Do you meditate just to become receptive to psychic experiences? No. Meditation is totally independent of psychic phenomena. It is a tool, however, in helping to develop psychic abilities. It also serves as a clearing of the child's mind, making it easier for him or he to focus on studies and work. During meditation frustrations are minimized and anxieties lessened. In clearing his mind, the child will gradually become more receptive to psychic happenings. Meditation helps in the disciplining of the child's energies but in a manner separate and apart from concentrated methods; it also gives him organization, enabling him to tackle his tasks in an orderly manner without losing time or expending unnecessary energy.

There are many other possible forms of meditation. The three simplified suggestions above will guide readers in helping children to adapt to the meditation process in an interesting and pleasant fashion. In providing a child with understanding and a pleasant, relaxed environment, parents will see their child's psychic awareness flourish.

A twelve-year-old boy on a camping trip in the mountains became separated from the rest of his group. He was lost for nine days and was feared to be dead. He knew enough to eat berries, drink water, and follow water downstream. When he was found, on the tenth day, hungry and exhausted, he was asked how he had survived the ordeal. The boy said that each night, just before he fell asleep, he heard his mother's voice calming him, telling him not to be afraid and to be sure and get the rest he needed. Her voice offered solace and encouragement to go on and win the fight to survive in the woods. This continued every night that he was lost. His mother, at the same time, was sending prayers for survival to her son, urging him to get rest and not to be afraid. The boy heard these, and the telepathic communications from his mother during this stressful time helped him to survive the harrowing experience.

Later, as an officer in the navy during a World War II battle in the Java Sea, he was again in a position of survival and again heard a voice that told him he would overcome the danger and be saved. He later learned that his mother had felt he was in great danger at that time and had been fervently praying for his safety. He had a similar experience during the Korean War.

The psychic awareness made manifest at the early age of twelve stood this boy in good stead the rest of his life. To this day, the man credits many of the important decisions he has made throughout his life to his psychic ability to receive messages.

We see time and time again that psychic abilities can be expressed in many ways and can be integrated into everyday life, as the following example indicates.

A young boy had lost his wallet, but he heard his father, who was taking an ESP course, say that lost objects may be found through psychic ability. The boy thought about this and then sat in a chair. After about five minutes, he jumped up and told his father he had seen the wallet under a pillow in the couch at his friend's house. He checked, and there was the wallet.

What have we here? It is true that the boy could have suddenly "remembered" where the wallet had been lost. If so, he certainly had to remember a great many places where he might have lost it, for he had been that day to the grocery store, to a movie, out in the backyard, etc. However, there are advantages to utilizing a psychic approach to this problem. The entire thesis behind teaching a child to use his psychic abilities is to help solve problems in his life and to exercise his creativity. In this instance, the boy did both. By grasping the creative approach his father wished him to follow, he was able to use it constructively in a problem-solving fashion. The technique was certainly something he could utilize in his future.

Suppose you want to teach your child history, but he thinks it's boring. You might find a clue among the things that already interest him. For example, if he is interested in trains, you might give him a book on the *history of trains*, which could lead to an understanding and appreciation of history in general. A well-developed interest is not narrowly circumscribed but spreads across the boundaries of other interests. With innovative ESP tests and games serving to stimulate a child's interest, psychic abilities may be compared to the history book on trains. Psychic development can be used to foster the creativity of a child, broadening his interests and making him a more well-rounded individual. The child will have a greater awareness of the world around him and at the same time will be able to daydream.

In spontaneous discussions at the dinner table parents can inquire: "What do you want in life? Can you ever achieve it? Have you got the ability for it? If you do, *will it*, and by willing it, all the forces will come to you to help you succeed." This is the culmination of the daydream. It is also the scope of vision with which psychic awareness provides a child—the insight to see what he or she wants, be it long-term or short-term. By "long-term" or "short-term," we mean does he need it next week or several weeks after? The more general the better, because the mind will follow the direction of his goal, and indecision is eliminated. Once a child *wills* what he wants, he should not change his mind, because it will interfere with the psychic reaching out for the aid he is seeking. Parents should encourage their child to utilize his psychic awareness to help him achieve his desires. The child should be taught to feel secure in his decisions: "Make sure that what you want is really what you want. If it is, you must *will it* rather than think how nice it would be. You must will it with the realization that you won't change your mind. Then the psychic forces will bring you all the things you'll need and put them in your pathway to success. You'll still have to work at it, but your psychic awareness will help you make the right choice." The child gains confidence and is able to make decisions that he sticks to without wavering, and is on his way to achieving his goal.

Here is a simplified example of what we have just said: You are walking along the street, thinking of someone. For no reason you enter a store, and there you see the person of whom you were thinking. How did you both happen to be at the same place at the same time? The forces were brought into play consciously or unconsciously. We have taught this in our parapsychology courses to more than two thousand students. The majority of the responses and feedback was that this application of psychic awareness had been very successful. This is what we should teach children in order to give them a vision of what they really want in life, to give children *total* development. *In this book, we are relating the psychic experience to a child's ability to seek success for himself—and providing him with the opportunity. After all, what else do you want for your child but for him to succeed in life in a healthy and happy way?*

Part Three

Tests and Games
for Developing
Psychic Abilities

Nine

Test Information and Instructions for Parents and Teachers

These ESP tests are given not with a scientific approach but rather with the understanding that we are only trying to discover and enhance the natural psychic abilities of children. The tests are *not* to be conducted under stringent laboratory conditions but are to be presented to children in a gamelike atmosphere in the classroom with a teacher, in the home with a parent, or with another child. Psychic abilities are like any other ability children have, like that used to excel in sports, music, drawing, and so on. In no event should a child's status be elevated as the result of high scoring; instead, his psychic ability should be treated as a natural one. It should be explained that these are simply games. A child may do better at one than another. Some children score higher in telepathy, others in clairvoyance.

Let's pause here for a moment and examine the importance of testing children for ESP and some of the primary purposes:

- To try to determine if the child has psychic ability.
- To exercise that ability so the child can utilize his psychic talent as a creative tool in his everyday life, just as you would

want a child to practice if he displayed ability in baseball or music.

- To help serve as a barometer in analyzing the relationships between teacher and student, parent and child.

The tests are structured to indicate a child's degree of psychic ability. The first ten tests given in any one category should be used to establish an average base, which can then be used as a standard for future developments.

The same tests (with variations) should be continued over a period of time so that the children do not tire. The procedure you follow should be geared to fit children's special needs. For example, a few short tests may prove to be a better way of obtaining results than one long session. The length of each test will best be determined by individual situations, but if you limit the testing to between half an hour and an hour, you will probably succeed in holding the children's attention. Younger children have short attention spans, so the tester will have to decide when to break off the test period.

As children of all ages are highly conscious of tests, it must be stressed again that the tests should be treated as a game. In testing for psychic abilities, children should be relaxed and at ease to obtain favorable results. In many of the tests, other than pencils and score sheets, an ordinary deck of playing cards is the only equipment needed. Cards are simple and are usually found around the house. Children are receptive to a game of cards and will readily participate.

Since the test is treated as a game, children will usually want to know their scores, and they should be allowed to know them if they wish. However, also explain that scores can vary from day to day. In looking for ways to minimize stress, you may find it helpful to allow the children to participate in some fashion other than the actual guessing. For example, they might take turns distributing papers or pencils. A brief period of meditation prior to testing will be helpful in creating a relaxed atmosphere (see Chapter 8).

There are no ideal conditions. Many variables may create an atmosphere for either higher or lower scoring. It has been noticed in professional testing that there are certain points when a child may reach a very high score and other times when his score may decline. Decline should not become an issue. Some of this fluctuation may be attributed to trying too hard, fatigue, the attitude of the parent or teacher, the mood of the child himself—or the loss of interest because the child was pushed. Everyone has an off day.

Douglas Dean of the Newark College of Engineering, coauthor of *Executive ESP*, believes that there is a link between stress and the ability to score well on ESP tests. He observed this first when a student from whom he anticipated good results produced extremely poor ones. The boy told Dean that he had a stiff exam the next day and that he was very concerned about it. Dean came to the conclusion that "ESP goes negative when you're 'uptight.' Any sort of psychological or physiological stress appears to turn off intuition." The hypothesis put forth by Dean—that there are stress barriers associated with ESP responses and that physiological and/or psychological stress interferes with the reception of ESP signals—is of concern to us. If children do not score well on their ESP tests, this does not necessarily indicate that they don't have ESP ability; rather, it may indicate that the psi-negative factor is operating.

In talking to teachers about tests, their fallibility, and the need for the teacher's own resources, we should pay special heed to Dr. Louisa E. Rhine:

It seems that everyone has psi ability, but like the ability to sing, though every normal person can do it, some do it better and easier than others. Singing, however, can be improved by proper teaching, but for psi no teachers yet know the rules. It is a spontaneous, natural gift, like humor. Any rules for how to tell a joke can only help a little. It is something a few people "just know" and others never learn.[1]

It should be remembered that all psychic abilities vary from time to time. The same test taken another day may reveal completely different results. These tests are *not* being conducted under scientific laboratory conditions, and the test results, compared to pure chance, are merely suggestive of the psychic ability of any one child. We are attempting to discover if a child does have psychic ability; we are *not* trying to establish the statistical reliability of test figures.

To show how results can vary, let's look at two experiences told to us in a recent letter from school psychologist Eloise Shields:

> Susie was a peppy, lively 10-year-old youngster whom I was testing for her balking at the teacher's authority. She *loved* to come for testing, and spent much time chatting about her life and interests. The day I brought out the ESP test, she was interested in it, but not as much as in talking. So we ran through the demonstration, then proceeded into the actual test. This was the Matching Abacus Test, which I run through five times with each child. She had done it four times, with no correct answers so far (which is quite rare). Then suddenly she stopped talking and inquired, "How many of these things do other kids get right?" I explained that five was a pretty high score. And sure enough, the last time around she made 5 out of 10 correct, which is *extremely* rare. She apparently did this on purpose, using her clairvoyance and psi ability to produce *when she wanted to.*

Susie was able to score "when she wanted to"—when her spirit of competitiveness was aroused. Also, after four times around, Susie may have felt that in order to return to the talking, which she loved, it would be wise to stop the testing process. Possibly she had earlier thought the easiest road to this end was an unusual act (no score at all) to get the teacher's attention. Or, because she had been sent to Mrs. Shields for balking at a teacher's authority, perhaps she was simply displaying her temperament: She would not score on the teacher's authority but only on her own say-so, which she proceeded to do on the fifth trial run!

Mrs. Shields tells of an example of how too much praise can prove detrimental:

Another [child] I tested, named Tim, was a seventh-grader who was a non-reader, new to our school, and the principal asked for some testing to see where to place him. He had average intelligence, but could only read at the first-grade level. When I pulled out the ESP test, he was interested, helpful in setting it up, and curious about this new and interesting, non-academic test. I demonstrated how to do it, then proceeded with the test itself. The very first time around, he got 5 out of 10 correct (quite exceptional). Then I praised him profusely. He never got another one right!! I later realized that here was a boy who had consistently failed in school in everything he had done so far. Yet here was a psychologist, telling him he was *good* at something. He just couldn't fit this in with his failure "set" about school, and went back to the old failure syndrome. I soon learned, from that experience, not to be too full of praise with some children or it might scare them into retreating into their failure syndrome.

Researchers Athena Drewes and Sally Ann Drucker advise that children make excellent ESP subjects because they are open to new experiences. They suggest that some researchers may benefit from practical suggestions gained from their experiments with children's ESP:

> Children want tangible or edible rewards to see how much they've won by correct guessing. We used colorful M&M's candies (one of each color) as targets and found this very successful in maintaining attention span; children participated enthusiastically in a "game" that provided immediate literal feedback! At the end, so that no child would be disappointed at not winning anything, we always gave them the five demonstration M&M's.
>
> It's also important to establish a peaceful, relaxed environment. We found that children tested at home scored higher than those tested in a nursery-day-care situation. The cooperation of the family (parents and siblings) is vital. If candy is to be used, ask permission of parents, as they may disapprove [of] the consumption or fear it could spoil dinner appetites. If messy material is being used, be sure to conduct the test where it won't damage furnishings. If siblings are likely to disrupt the study, arrange for them to participate later when the actual test is over, or give them a treat, too; this will help eliminate rivalry and assuage curiosity.
>
> Personality differences can affect the scoring of children. . . . Withdrawn children score significantly lower than nonwithdrawn. As with adults, children who are "believers" achieve higher scores than nonbelievers, nonbelievers even showing psi-missing. However, very young children haven't fully accepted the cultural inhibitions about ESP. Thus, the 4- to 9-year-olds we worked with never seemed to feel that a guessing game couldn't work. If they won only a few M&M's, they apparently just concluded they were poor guessers.

Younger students seem to excel at telepathy, older ones at clairvoyance. This may be related to the younger child's higher dependency on the teacher and the older one's growing need for independence.[2]

The smaller the group, the better (obviously, some teachers will have more students than others). However, there is no reason to be overly concerned, as a significant degree of success has been achieved with large groups as well.

In other tests, an interesting note was discovered, one of considerable importance for both teachers and parents and for the teaching profession in general. This was a finding unearthed in tests by former teacher Miss Rhea White and her colleague Miss Margaret Anderson, both of whom were interested in ESP in the schoolroom. Together with J. G. Van Dusschbach, a school superintendent in the Netherlands who was invited to the Duke Parapsychology Laboratory in the United States, experiments were conducted by testing twenty-three fifth- and sixth-grade classes and seventeen seventh- and eighth-grade classes in two American cities. Results revealed that the personal liking of the student for the teacher and of the teacher for the student had a bearing on the outcome of the ESP tests. In an attempt to evaluate this finding further, the teachers were asked to rate their feeling for each student. The students were then asked to rate the way they felt about their teacher. In order to assure the children that teachers would not see their responses, all of the ratings were sealed and mailed to Miss Anderson and Miss White.

Dr. Louisa Rhine took a look at the ratings:

These ratings produced four groups of relationships among the students: 1. those who liked the teacher and were liked by her; 2. those who disliked the teacher and were disliked by her;

3. and 4. groups that combined like-dislike attitudes. The results were that ESP scores were highest in the mutual likers (1) and lowest in the mutual dislikers (2). These last were so far below the chance level that they . . . *avoided* the targets more than they could have done by chance alone.

Later, Anderson and White correlated the ESP scores with the students' attitudes toward the teacher and with their class grades. In general this showed that the higher the student's grades, the higher his ESP score too. Of course, the attitude of the teacher to a pupil probably affected his grade, but the ESP score was an independent measure.

Most interesting of all was the fact that the children who received low class grades and whom the teacher did not like had ESP scores regularly below chance. It looked as though the student–teacher attitude, which of course was linked with the class grades, was disclosed in the ESP test itself. Thus, the ESP result could serve, in a way, as an indicator of teacher–student relations.[3]

Similar tests began to take place in countries all over the world. In France, Madame Christiane Vasse, a primary-school teacher in Amiens, conducted an experiment to see if the importance of good rapport between teacher and pupils in her class of first-grade children could be shown. We relate this particular teacher's decision to conduct these tests to show her tremendous innovative ability in obtaining her goal. The French school system does not permit a teacher to introduce an outside project such as an ESP test during school hours. Madame Vasse worked with the children, only those who wanted to play "the ESP game," at recess period, and ultimately was able to show that the ESP demonstrated by the schoolchildren was heavily dependent on the pupil-teacher relationship.

These same attitudes can possibly also be established between parent and child when testing for ESP at home. Madame Vasse's creative idea of working with the children at recess enabled her to work with the children in a relaxed atmosphere and to treat the tests in a gamelike fashion. Similarly, to obtain good results either in the classroom or at home, the ingenuity and sincere interest of the person conducting the tests will have a great bearing on the outcome. Time and time again, researchers have indicated that when skepticism, disbelief, or disinterest creeps into tests, the subject, whether child or adult, does not score well.

Ten

Instructions and Tests for Telepathy

Purpose of Tests

In this chapter, we will be testing for telepathy, a way to send or receive thought messages of any kind from one person to another. Telepathy is the awareness of someone else's thoughts at the moment he or she is thinking them.

Method

The first step will be for the tester to give each child an ESP scoring sheet and a pencil. (Several types of scoring sheets are included at the end of Chapter 12.) The Standard Score Sheet will be used unless otherwise indicated. The next step is for the tester to shuffle the cards, being careful to make sure that none of the children see the face values. The tester will then choose a card and look at it (without any of the children seeing it). Announcing "Target," the tester will concentrate on the chosen card for four or five seconds. During those few seconds, the children will write down their first spontaneous impression of the card. While it would be pleasant to permit the children to work at their own speed, spontaneity is a vital factor in testing for ESP. Dalliance must be avoided, whether testing with a group in the classroom or with one child at home.

A show of raised hands when all are finished acts as a good indicator of when to proceed to the next call.

Timing

Since each test run of twenty-five calls will take approximately five minutes to complete, it is advisable for the teacher to do no more than four tests of the same type (totaling 100 trials) at any one sitting. Score sheets will have columns for a total of four separate "call runs."

Scoring

Samples of score sheets, together with samples of symbols or objects, appear at the end of Chapter 12. Children may be told their score, but only at the end of each complete run, and no "second-guessing" is permitted. And remember: No undue praise for excellence!

In order to establish a base for a particular child's psychic ability in telepathy or any of the other ESP talents, a minimum of ten tests should be administered to come up with an average. There can be fairly wide variances in the scoring of any one child, and it is only over a period of time that an actual trend may be observed. The base period of ten tests is important in establishing the future progress of a child's psychic ability. It will be used as a check for future tests.

Be sure to let the children know that these scores are not like numbers or grades in a history or mathematics test and therefore will be scored differently. Because children may not readily understand a numerical score of 2 or 16, it will be helpful to them if the tester uses a system of scoring involving gummed seals or stars. In this way, the tester can easily apply a score to each child's sheet by affixing a star. A gold star can indicate the highest score, silver the next highest, then blue, green, or red. Thus, *every child receives a star*. (This method can be modified by using any type of seals, such as fruits, animals, flowers, or other symbols, as long as the seals being used are the same throughout the tests and *as long as every child receives a seal of some type*.) If you have a box of seals or stars that are all of the same kind, you may still improvise by giving two, three, or four of the stars or seals on the score sheet to indicate the grade or mark.

Instructions for evaluating the score sheets will be given at the end of each test. The "standard" score sheet will apply to each test unless otherwise designated. The test results (as compared to pure chance) are merely suggestive of the psychic ability that any one child has.

Telepathy Test 1

The Thought Test of 0 and 1

EQUIPMENT NEEDED
• Pencils and score sheets

INSTRUCTIONS
• Score sheets and pencils are distributed to the children as well as to the tester.
• The tester tells the children that he is going to think of a number and that it will be either zero (0) or one (1).
• After the tester announces "Target," the children will have approximately 5 seconds to guess the number he is thinking.
• After all the children have entered their responses in the appropriate column, the tester writes the number in the Target column of his score sheet.

- The same procedure is followed until 25 trials have been made.
- It is important that the tester try to vary the numbers called, lest a pattern be established that the children may recognize. It should be a spontaneous thought-call on the part of the tester.
- Nothing should be prepared in the way of written material in advance for the tester to call from. If he were to do that, he would be testing for clairvoyance or precognition.
- After 25 calls have been made, the tester will proceed to the next call run of 25 tries until a total of 100 is reached.
- Score sheets are handed to the tester at the end of the test period.

SCORING AND EVALUATION

The average score to be expected from pure chance is 50 percent, or 50 hits per run of 100 trials. In other words, if a child gets 50 correct guesses out of 100, this would be based on pure chance expectation. Correct guesses of 60 or more would be significant and beyond chance.

Telepathy Test 2

The Red and Blue Thought Test

EQUIPMENT NEEDED
- Pencils and score sheets

INSTRUCTIONS
- The tester explains to the children that he will think of a color, either red or blue.
- After the tester announces "Target," the children are to guess what color the tester is thinking of and write their answer

in the Response column of their score sheet: "R" for red, "B" for blue.

- When all the children have entered their responses (approximately 5 seconds is allowed), the tester then writes the color in the Target column of his score sheet.
- The same procedure is followed until 25 trials have been made.
- The tester should try to avoid patterns in calling, such as "red, blue, red, blue, red, blue." It should be a spontaneous thought-call on the part of the tester.
- The tester should not write down his calls before the test. If he were to do that, he would then be testing for clairvoyance or precognition.
- After 25 calls, the tester will proceed to the next call run of 25 tries until a total of 100 is reached.
- Score sheets are handed to the tester at the end of the test period.

SCORING AND EVALUATION

The average score to be expected from pure chance alone is 50 percent, or 50 hits per run of 100 trials. Correct guesses of 60 or more would be significant and beyond chance.

Telepathy Test 3

The East–West Thought Test

EQUIPMENT NEEDED

- Pencils and score sheets

INSTRUCTIONS

- The tester tells the children that he is going to think of a direction, either east or west.

- The children are to identify the thought impression they receive as either "E" or "W," and upon the tester's announcing "Target," the children will have approximately 5 seconds to guess which direction he is thinking of.
- After all the children have entered their responses in the appropriate column, the tester writes the direction in the Target column of his score sheet.
- The same procedure is followed until 25 trials have been made.
- The tester should try to vary the thinking of "east" or "west" to avoid establishing a pattern.
- The tester must *not* write down any calls in advance; if so, the test would then be for clairvoyance or precognition.
- After 25 calls have been made, the tester proceeds to the next call run of 25 tries until a total of 100 is reached.
- Score sheets are handed to the tester at the end of the test period.

SCORING AND EVALUATION

The average score to be expected from pure chance alone is 50 percent, or 50 hits per run of 100 trials. Correct guesses of 60 or more would be significant and beyond chance.

Telepathy Test 4

Basic Red- and Black-Card Test

EQUIPMENT NEEDED

- Ordinary deck of playing cards
- Pencils and score sheets

INSTRUCTIONS

- Score sheets and pencils are distributed to the children as well as to the tester.

- The tester tells the children he is going to think of the color of the card he selects, and they are to try and guess whether he is thinking of red or black.

- If the children think the tester is thinking of a red card, they should mark the letter R in the Response column of the score sheet. If they think the card is black, they should enter a B. It should be stressed that they are not to be concerned with the number of the card, only the color.

- The tester shuffles the deck of cards and places them facedown on a table or desk in front of him. The children should not be able to see the cards from where they are sitting.

- The tester then selects the first card, announces "Target," and thinks of the color for 5 to 7 seconds. After the children have all entered their responses, the tester enters the target color in the Target column on his score sheet.

- Prior to selecting the next card, the tester says to the children, "Ready for the next target now," and thinks of the next card he has turned up, again for 5 to 7 seconds. The turned-up cards are not shown to the children until the test is over.

- The same procedure is continued until 25 cards have been picked off the top of the deck.

- The tester then puts the 25 cards back into the original deck and reshuffles the pack, after which 25 more calls are made, using the same procedure as above. These responses on the second call run will be entered in column 2 of the score sheet. The four columns allow for a total of 100 trials.

- At the end of the test period, score sheets are handed to the tester.

The average score to be expected from pure chance alone is 50 percent, or 50 hits per run of 100 trials. Correct guesses of 60 or more would be significant and beyond chance.

Telepathy Test 5

Jack–and–Ace Test

EQUIPMENT NEEDED
- Four jacks and four aces are drawn from any ordinary deck of cards. The other cards are not used in this particular test.
- Pencils and score sheets

INSTRUCTIONS
- The Jack-and-Ace Test is a variation of the red and black color test (Test 4), the prime difference being that we are now testing for the face value of the card rather than its color. In the Response column, the children will put either *J* or *A*.
- Otherwise, the procedure is the same as that for Test 4. The tester shuffles the 8 cards, selects the first card, and looks at it. The tester then announces "Target" and silently concentrates on the face value of the card for approximately 5 seconds.
- After the children have entered their responses in the Response column, the tester enters the card under the Target column of his score sheet and proceeds to select another card. He then says aloud, "Ready for next target now," and proceeds to think of the second card he has selected from the top of the 8 cards, announcing "Target."
- After the 8 cards are disposed of, they are reshuffled, and the same procedure is continued for 24 trials (or 3 call runs of the

8 cards). When this has been completed, the tester reshuffles the eight jacks and aces and repeats the calls for a total of 25 tries.

- The same procedure is followed for a total of 100 trials. (There are four columns, allowing 25 trials each.)
- Score sheets are handed to the tester following the test period.

SCORING AND EVALUATION

The average score by chance alone is 50 percent, or 50 hits per run of 100 trials. Correct guesses of 60 or more would be significant and beyond chance.

Telepathy Test 6

The Twenty-five-Card-Run Test (for Older Children)

EQUIPMENT NEEDED
- Ordinary deck of playing cards
- Pencils and score sheets

INSTRUCTIONS
- Score sheets and pencils are distributed to the children as well as to the tester.
- The tester shuffles the deck and, without looking at the face value, counts off the first 25 cards, placing them facedown. The rest of the deck is put aside.
- In this test, children are told that their response will indicate *both* the numerical value *and* the suit of the card. The letters to be used for responses are: C (clubs), S (spades), H (hearts), and D (diamonds). The response for the 10 of diamonds card would be "10 D," and should be written in the Response column of

the score sheet. (This may require a few demonstrations to be sure the children understand the instructions.)

- The tester selects the first card and looks at it. He then announces "Target" and proceeds to concentrate on the face value and suit for 5 to 7 seconds.
- After the children have entered their responses in the Response column, the tester enters the card in the Target column of his score sheet and proceeds to select another card. The tester then says aloud, "Ready for next target now." Upon announcing "Target," he thinks about the color and face value of the second card. This procedure is continued with the 25 remaining cards.
- At the end of the first 25-card run, the entire deck is reshuffled by the tester and 25 more cards are taken off the top in the same manner as above. This is repeated until four complete runs, totaling 100 trials, have been completed.
- Score sheets are turned in to the tester, who must remember when scoring this test that there will be "partial hits" or "full hits." A partial hit may consist of either the number *or* the suit. A full hit, of course, is the number *and* the suit.

SCORING AND EVALUATION

The scoring of this test is a bit more intricate. We are attempting only to discover if a child has some degree of psychic ability. The scoring will be 2 points for a full hit, 1 point for a numerical hit, and $^1/_2$ point for a suit hit. In other words:

- To guess the *suit* is 1 out of 4 chances (25 out of 100 is pure chance) and is worth $^1/_2$ point in scoring.
- To guess the *number* is 1 out of 13 chances (8 in 100 is pure chance) and is worth 1 point in scoring.

- To guess both number and suit is 1 out of 52 chances (2 out of 100 is chance) and is worth 2 points in scoring.

In the total of 100 trials (with the above scoring), a score of 29 or more could be considered significant. The higher the tally, the more strongly telepathic ability is indicated.

Telepathy Test 7

The Five-Object Test (See Five-Object Score Sheet)

SPECIAL NOTE

This test is geared to children ages five to seven. However, younger children may participate if they can write the letters of the alphabet. The Five-Object Test may be modified for older children by using more sophisticated objects, such as a football, a bicycle, or whatever else is representative of their interests. Older children may enjoy selecting their own target objects for the test.

EQUIPMENT NEEDED

- Five sheets of paper or five blank index cards of any size
- Cardboard to be used as backing if you can see through paper or cards
- Black crayon or any type of felt-tipped pen or marking pencil
- Pencils and score sheets

PREPARATION FOR TEST

- On each of the five cards or sheets of paper, either draw five objects or paste their pictures. (See samples of five typical objects in the illustrations at the end of Chapter 12 as well as the related Five-Object Score Sheet.)

In this test, we have elected to use the following objects:

APPLE	BANANA	CAR	DUCK	ELEPHANT
A	B	C	D	E

- The children will use the letters A through E to indicate their responses.
- The tester may copy or trace the illustrations and the score sheets for tests in the classroom or at home, but this material may not be used for publication purposes of any kind. It is important to remember that the children must not be able to see through the paper when it is viewed from the back. If the illustration can be seen, paste or staple the target sheets to a cardboard backing.
- We have incorporated an optional step into the score sheet for this test. (See Five-Object Score Sheet at the end of Chapter 12.) The five target objects have been sketched in miniature form to assist the children in spontaneous responses with the appropriate identifying alphabetical lettering shown underneath each object. While we recommend the use of the Five-Object Score Sheet, you may also use the Standard ESP Score Sheet should you prefer.

INSTRUCTIONS

- Before beginning the test, the tester shows the five target objects to the children and identifies each object as being the same as those appearing on their scoring sheet. (The latter is done only if pictures are indicated on the score sheets. Otherwise, simply identify the five objects being used as targets.)
- The tester shuffles the five cards and lays them down in a row in front of him in any pattern, for they are to be selected at random.

- The tester tells the children he will select one object at a time and asks them to concentrate while he is thinking of the target object. He also tells them to write their first impression on the score sheet. Remind them that the alphabetical letters A, B, C, D, and E are to be used as their responses.
- Allow 5 to 7 seconds for responses to be made, after which the tester enters the target object on his score sheet in the Target column.
- The tester then announces, "Ready for next object," and after a second or two says "Target," and proceeds to think for 5 to 7 seconds about the second card selected. This procedure continues until 25 trials have been made. (Because older children have a longer attention span, the test can go on to a second, third, and fourth run-through until 100 trials have been completed. To achieve 100 trials on this test for younger children, it is probably best to continue the second run at another time. This also applies to third- and fourth-call runs.)

SCORING AND EVALUATION
- Score sheets are handed to the tester for scoring.
- Chance would be 5 out of 25. Conducting the four run-throughs for a total of 100 trials is the best way to establish a trend. Out of 100, chance would be 25. A score of 30 or more could be considered significant.

Eleven

Clairvoyance
Tests

Purpose of Test

To test for clairvoyant ability, which is the ability to perceive distant images, symbols, or events without the use of any of the known physical senses. The child is able to "see" a hidden card or symbol without anyone else seeing or looking at it.

Method

The most important thing to remember is that *under no circumstances is the tester to see the card or symbol being used once the test has commenced.* The tester's function is that of interested bystander. Once the test has started and the children have given their responses, the tester will then be permitted to look at the "target" material and enter it on the score sheet.

During the various clairvoyance tests, it is the job of the tester to announce "target" at each call. A period of 5 to 7 seconds should be allowed for indicating a "response," that is, the children's impression of the target. While it would be pleasant to permit children to work at their own speed, spontaneity is a vital factor in testing for ESP. Dalliance must be avoided, whether testing with a group in the classroom or with one child at home. A show of raised hands when all are finished is a good indicator of when to proceed to the next call.

After all of the children have entered their responses, the tester then—*and only then*—looks at the object being tested by turning it faceup, whether it be a card or a symbol. At this point the tester enters the name of the "target" on his score sheet in the appropriate column. The children should not sit within view of the target material.

Timing

Each test run (of 25 calls each) should take less than 10 minutes to complete. Score sheets will have columns for a total of four separate "call runs," and it is suggested that no more than four runs of the same test be conducted at any one sitting. It is left to the tester to determine the exact number of call runs; the children's attention span will help him or her to decide whether to have more than one or two. If interest wanes, one run may be preferable to four.

Scoring

Samples of score sheets, together with samples of symbols or objects, appear at the end of Chapter 12. Children may be told their score, but only at the end of each complete run, and no "second-guessing" is permitted. And remember: no undue praise for excellence! Let the children know that these scores are not like numbers or grades in a history or mathematics test and therefore will be scored differently.

For those wishing to observe long-term results, a minimum of ten tests should be given to establish an average base for a child. This is particularly important because there can be wide variances in a child's scoring, as explained in Chapter 9. It is only over a period of time that any trend can be determined. Therefore, it is vital to have a base period of approximately ten tests in order to establish the progress of a child's psychic ability. The base period should be used as a check for future tests.

Instructions for evaluating the score sheets will be given at the end of each test. The "standard" score sheet will apply to each test unless otherwise designated. The test results (as compared to pure chance) are merely suggestive of the psychic ability that any one child has.

Clairvoyance Test 1

Basic Red-versus-Black—Card Test

EQUIPMENT NEEDED
- Ordinary deck of playing cards
- Pencils and score sheets

INSTRUCTIONS
- Score sheets and pencils are distributed to the children as well as to the tester.
- The tester tells the children to try to guess whether a card is red or black by concentrating on it.
- If they think the card is red, the children should write the letter R in the Response column of the score sheet. If they think the card is black, they should enter a B in that column. The

children should understand that they are not to be concerned with the face value but only with the color of the card.

- The tester shuffles the deck of cards and places them facedown before him on a desk or table. The children should not be able to view the cards from where they are sitting.
- The tester then asks the children to "see" what color the first card is and announces, "Target 1." *The tester does not look at the card.* (To look at the card would change it to a telepathic test.) The tester then proceeds to announce "Target 2," "Target 3," etc.
- Allow 5 to 7 seconds for the children to enter their responses on the score sheet. Afterward, the tester turns the target card faceup and sees it for the first time. The tester enters the color of the card on his score sheet. The turned-up card is not shown to the children until the test is over.
- The same procedure is followed until 25 cards have been picked off the top of the deck.
- The tester then puts the 25 cards back into the original deck and reshuffles the pack, after which 25 more calls are made, following the same procedure as above. These responses will be entered under column 2 of the score sheet. The same procedure is followed for columns 3 and 4. The four columns allow for a total of 100 trials.
- The score sheets are handed to the tester at the end of the test period.

SCORING AND EVALUATION

The average score to be expected from pure chance is 50 percent, or 50 hits per run of 100 trials. Correct guesses of 60 or more would be significant and beyond chance.

Clairvoyance Test 2

Guess the Number

EQUIPMENT NEEDED
- Ordinary deck of playing cards
- Pencils and score sheets

INSTRUCTIONS
- Score sheets and pencils are distributed to the children as well as to the tester.
- The tester removes all face cards (jacks, queens, and kings). With the ace acting as the number 1, this leaves 40 numerical cards. Children should be advised of the value of the ace. Only 25 of the 40 cards are called.
- The children are told not to worry about color, just numerical value.
- The tester asks the children to concentrate on the card and try to "see" in their mind's eye what the number is. If they think it is an ace, the children should put the number 1 into the Response column. If they think the card is a 10, the children should insert that number in the Response column, and so on.
- The tester must not look at the target card until the children have entered their responses, so as not to change the nature of the test to telepathy.
- The tester shuffles the 40-card deck and places it on a desk or table before him. Children should not be able to see the cards from where they are sitting.
- After the tester announces "Target," the children enter their response. After 5 to 7 seconds have elapsed and the children

have entered their responses, the tester turns the card faceup, seeing it for the first time. He enters the number in the Target column on his score sheet. The turned-up card is not shown to the children until the test is over.

- The deck of 40 cards is reshuffled by the tester and the same procedure is followed until 25 more calls have been made.
- The tests should be repeated for a total of four runs—100 trials—after which score sheets should be turned in to the tester for scoring.

SCORING AND EVALUATION

The average score to be expected from chance alone is 10 percent, or 10 hits per run of 100 trials. Correct guesses of 16 or more would be highly significant and well beyond chance.

Clairvoyance Test 3

Random Five-Card Choice (for Older Children)

EQUIPMENT NEEDED
- Ordinary deck of playing cards
- Pencils and score sheets

INSTRUCTIONS
- Score sheets and pencils are distributed to the children as well as to the tester.
- The tester shuffles the deck. Without looking at any of the cards, the tester selects five at random. These five are placed in individual rows in front of the tester. (Children sit out of view of target cards.)
- Before this test, the children are told that their response will

indicate both the numerical value and the suit of the card. S represents spades, C clubs, D diamonds, and H hearts. The response for the 10 of diamonds would be "10 D."

- The tester explains to the children that he will point to each of the five cards in front of him in turn, proceeding from left to right.

- After the tester calls "Target," the children are to "see" what each card is and write their responses on the score sheets. Approximately 7 seconds is allowed for response. (In marking the response, the number is to be indicated first and then the suit: "10 D.")

- Upon completion of the first call run of five cards, the tester turns the five cards faceup and sees them for the first time. The tester enters them on his score sheet from 1 to 5 (the left to right sequence of calling the targets).

- The entire deck is reshuffled by the tester, and five more cards are picked at random. The same procedure as above is followed until 25 calls are made. (In other words, the tester is selecting 5 cards 5 times for a total of 25 calls.)

- This is repeated and the test run of 25 calls continues for four complete runs, totaling 100.

- Score sheets are handed to the tester, who must remember when scoring this test that there will be "partial hits" or "full hits." A partial hit may consist of either the number *or* the suit. A full hit, obviously, is the number *and* the suit.

SCORING AND EVALUATION

Two points are given for a full hit, 1 point for a numerical hit, and $^1/_2$ point for a suit hit. In other words:

- To guess the suit is 1 out of 4 chances (25 out of 100 is pure chance) and is worth $^1/_2$ point in scoring.

- To guess the number is 1 out of 13 chances (8 in 100 is pure chance) and is worth 1 point in scoring.
- To guess both the number and the suit is 1 out of 52 chances (2 out of 100 is chance) and is worth 2 points in scoring.

In the total of 100 trials (with the above scoring), a score of 29 or more could be considered significant. The higher the tally, the more strongly clairvoyant ability is indicated.

Clairvoyance Test 4

Self-Administered Random Five-Card Choice Test (for Older Children)

EQUIPMENT NEEDED
- Ordinary deck of playing cards
- Pencils and score sheets

INSTRUCTIONS
- This test may be conducted with two children or with one child taking the test by himself or herself.
- The child shuffles a regular deck of playing cards.
- Without looking at any of the cards, he or she selects five of them at random and places them facedown in individual rows in front of him.
- The child looks at the back of each one of the cards, and within 5 to 7 seconds writes in the Response column what he thinks that particular card is. He continues from left to right, looking at each card in that sequence.
- After writing down each of the five guesses in the Response column on the score sheet, the child turns the cards over one by one (from left to right) and marks each in the Target column.

- This procedure is repeated five times, each time reshuffling the deck and randomly selecting five target cards. At the end of the first run there will be a total of 25 calls for scoring.
- The test may end now, or the child may continue until four columns of 25 calls each have been completed. As an alternative the player may wish to continue the test the next day and compare the 25 calls to the previous score. The same score sheet may be used until all four columns are completed.

SCORING AND EVALUATION
See Test 3 for scoring procedure and evaluation.

Clairvoyance Test 5

Where Is the Ace of Hearts?

EQUIPMENT NEEDED
- Ordinary deck of playing cards
- Pencils and score sheet

INSTRUCTIONS
- This is a test that a child can do alone or with a parent. One child can also do it with another.
- From the 52-card deck, take out the 2, 3, 4, 5, 6, 7, 8, and 9 of clubs. Also remove the ace of hearts, discarding all other cards. There are now nine cards to be used in the test.
- Shuffle the nine cards and lay all of them in single rows, facedown, in any pattern. The child should then look at the backs of the cards until an impression forms as to which card is the ace of hearts.
- The child starts to select cards, looking for the ace of hearts.

Each card is turned over after it is selected. If the child does not spot the ace of hearts on the first try, the test should continue until the ace of hearts shows up, at which point the test is discontinued. The child then goes on to Test 6.

- If the child spots the ace of hearts on the first go-round, the test is then discontinued and the child is to go on to Test 6.
- This test is discontinued after a first attempt because spontaneity is so important in testing for clairvoyance. Having seen the first results, the child may feel pressured by follow-up attempts, or too concentrated an effort may yield poor results. While this is not always the case, it is probably best to move along to Test 6, returning to Test 5 the next day. The child may continue with other ESP tests or games during that period, however.

SCORING AND EVALUATION

Scoring should consist of how many attempts are made until the ace of hearts appears. Average chance would be 1 out of 9. One out of 8 would still probably be chance.

A correct guess on the first try as to where the ace of hearts lies is a strong indication of clairvoyant ability. Clairvoyant ability is also present when a correct guess in locating the ace of hearts is made on the second, third, fourth, or fifth tries. Locating the ace in six or seven tries is borderline; while indicating some measure of clairvoyant ability, it is not very strong.

Clairvoyance Test 6

The Ace of Hearts Is Last

EQUIPMENT NEEDED
- Ordinary deck of playing cards
- Pencils and score sheets

- Like Test 5, this is a test that may be self-administered or given to the child by a parent. One child can also do it with another.
- Select the following cards from the deck: 2, 3, 4, 5, 6, 7, 8, and 9 of clubs. Also remove the ace of hearts, and set aside all other cards. There are now nine cards to be used.
- Shuffle the nine cards and lay them in single rows, facedown, in any pattern. The child should then look at the back of the cards and choose a card he thinks is a club. Then the card chosen should be turned over. The child continues looking for clubs, the purpose of the test being to turn over all of the clubs *before* finding the ace of hearts.
- As soon as the ace is found, the test is discontinued.
- As in Test 5, this test is discontinued after the first go-round, since spontaneity is important to the clairvoyance test. Follow-up attempts may yield poor results due to a more concentrated effort on the part of the child. Spontaneity is lost with too much concentrated repetition. While this is not always the case, it is probably best to move along to other types of tests and return to this one the next day.

SCORING AND EVALUATION

In Test 5, we were looking for one card—the ace of hearts. In this test, we are looking for all of the clubs in the first eight cards chosen—a more strenuous test. In other words, in looking for the ace of hearts in the previous test, in order to get a "hit," presumably only one guess could be needed. In this test, looking for all the clubs first, in order to get a hit one must guess eight times, so it is eight times the work.

Four clubs drawn first is pure chance. If the fifth card is a club, that is borderline. Six clubs or more drawn before the ace of hearts is found indicates strong clairvoyant ability.

Scoring should consist of the number of clubs turned over before the ace of hearts appeared. Remember again, psychic abilities may vary from time to time. The same test, taken another day, may show different results. A minimum of 10 tests should be given to establish an average base.

Clairvoyance Test 7

High-Card Test

EQUIPMENT NEEDED
- Ordinary deck of playing cards
- Pencils and score sheets

INSTRUCTIONS
- The tester must be sitting in the same position as that of the children, all facing forward. The tester then shuffles the cards.
- Holding the cards facedown, the tester divides them into three separate piles.
- The three piles of cards are called, from left to right, pile 1, pile 2, and pile 3.
- Without looking at any of the cards, the tester asks the children to try to "see" which of the three bottom cards is the highest. The ace ranks highest in this test.
- The children then write down their responses, indicating 1, 2, or 3 (representing the pile numbers) as having the highest card.
- The first guess having been made, the tester turns the three stacks of cards over to reveal the highest card on the bottom (*which the children do not see*) and enters the number in the Target column on his ESP score sheet.

- The tester reshuffles the cards and continues the same procedure until 25 calls have been made. The test is then repeated
for three more runs of 25 each, for a total of 100 trials. (It is
left to the tester to determine if two call runs or more should
be made at one sitting.)

SCORING AND EVALUATION

When there are 100 responses, the average score to be expected
by chance alone is 33–34. Anything above those figures would
be indicative of clairvoyance. The higher the number of correct
guesses, the greater the ability displayed.

Clairvoyance Test 8

Five-Object Test (See Five-Object Score Sheet.)

SPECIAL NOTE

This test is geared for children ages five to seven. However,
younger children may participate if they are able to write the
letters of the alphabet. The "Five-Object Test" may be modified
for older children by changing the objects used to more sophisticated ones. Older children may enjoy participating in selecting
their own target objects for the test, such as footballs, bicycles,
bridges, or whatever objects are representative of their interests.

EQUIPMENT NEEDED

- Five sheets of paper or five blank index cards of any size
- Cardboard (to be used as backing if you can see through the
paper or cards)
- Black crayon or any type of felt-tipped pen or marking pencil
- Pencils and score sheets

- On the five cards or sheets of paper either draw five objects, or paste pictures of objects on the cards. At the end of Chapter 12, see samples of five typical objects used, as well as the related score sheet.

  In this test, we have elected to use the following objects:

APPLE	BANANA	CAR	DUCK	ELEPHANT
A	B	C	D	E

- The tester may copy or trace either the illustrations or the score sheet for reproduction purposes for tests in the classroom or at home but not for publication purposes of any kind. It is important to remember that you must not be able to see through the paper when it is viewed from the back. If that is the case, paste or staple the target sheets to a cardboard backing.

- We have incorporated an optional step into the score sheet for this test. The five target objects have been sketched in miniature to assist the children in spontaneous responses with the appropriate identifying alphabetical lettering shown underneath each object.

INSTRUCTIONS

- Prior to beginning the test, the tester shows the five objects to the children and identifies each object as being the same as the one appearing on their score sheet (if sketches are indicated on the score sheets).

- The tester shuffles the five cards and lays them facedown in a row in front of him. The tester should be sitting in the same position as that of the children, that is, looking forward. He may sit in front, in back, or on the side, but the forward position must be maintained.

- The tester then tells the children that he will point to one object at a time from left to right and when he says "Target" the children are to tell their minds to "go under the card" and see what it is. Then they are to enter their response on the score sheet. The tester should allow approximately 5 to 7 seconds.

- After the children have all entered their responses for the five target calls, the tester turns the cards over, *seeing them for the first time,* and enters them in the Target column of his own score sheet.

- This is repeated four more times for a total of 25 trials. (For older children, the attention span may be longer, and the test can continue on to a second, third, and fourth run-through until 100 trials are reached. To achieve 100 trials on this test for younger children, it is probably best to continue the second run in the following test period. This also applies to third and fourth runs.)

SCORING AND EVALUATION

- Score sheets are handed to the tester for scoring.
- Chance would be 5 out of 25. Conducting the four run-throughs for a total of 100 trials is the best way to establish a trend. Out of 100, chance would be 25. A score of 30 or more could be considered significant.

Clairvoyance Test 9

Guess What's in the Picture

EQUIPMENT NEEDED

- A children's picture book or a magazine with pictures: A landscape scene of many objects (trees, river, sky, grass, cows, farm, house, boat, fisherman, ducks, a dog, etc.) is usually a good choice, but it may be any picture depicting any theme as long as there are many objects to identify.

- Paper and pencils

INSTRUCTIONS

- The tester takes the picture book or magazine and, without looking at its contents, opens it at random and lays it face-down so that neither the tester nor the children can see the pages.
- The children are asked to focus their mind's eye on the objects in the picture and to write down on paper whatever first impressions they receive.
- The test should not last more than 1 or 2 minutes; otherwise, a lot of guessing will take place. It is first impressions that are important here.
- At the end of a couple of minutes, the tester turns the picture book or magazine over, and the score sheets are handed to him.

SCORING AND EVALUATION

The closest one can come to scoring is a matter of noting how many objects the child can identify correctly. For example, if the picture shows a garden, the child might convey the impressions of flowers, trees, plants, grass, sky, ad infinitum. Obviously, if the child sees a garden with a fence around it, he doesn't need to see if there is a dog in the picture or rocks on the ground. In other words, if the picture depicts the garden with a fence around it and that is the child's response, that alone is enough to indicate clairvoyant ability, without any further details. Should more of the picture be "seen," it merely indicates the child was well focused on the target.

Twelve

Instructions and Tests for Other Psychic Abilities: Precognition, Psychometry, and Dowsing

PRECOGNITION: The knowing or seeing of events that will take place in the future. In the tests for precognition, children will guess a day in advance how the cards will fall when selected by the tester the next day.

PSYCHOMETRY: Touching or feeling an object and gaining thereby an impression of something of the history of the object or of those connected with it. In psychometry tests, let's remember that this particular psychic ability can consist of other ESP talents such as telepathy, clairvoyance, retrocognition, etc. Nonetheless, it is through the touch or the feeling of the object that the psychic impression is triggered.

DOWSING: A psychic talent used throughout the world and considered by many to be similar to psychometry. Many forms of dowsing rods are utilized, such as a stick with a forked end, a pendulum, a twig, etc. For the particular tests we are conducting, it is recommended that the tester use an inanimate object that can be constructed from a string and a small metal object or button for testing at home or in the classroom. (For how to use the other dowsing rods, see Chapter 1 and the explanation given under psychic terms.)

Precognition Test 1

Tomorrow's Red- or Black-Card Test

EQUIPMENT NEEDED
- Ordinary deck of playing cards
- Pencils and score sheets

INSTRUCTIONS
- The tester explains the nature of the test to the children: They are to guess how the cards will turn out when they are picked on the following day. The children are told only to think about the colors red and black, and not to worry about the number of the card.
- The children are then asked to write down, from 1 to 25 on the score sheet in the Response column, whether they think that card will come up red or black when it is picked the following day.
- Score sheets are given to the tester until the next day.
- On the day after the responses are written, the tester shuffles the deck of cards, and turns over the first 25 one by one. (The children may enjoy participating and may be allowed to take turns in turning over the cards.) The tester then enters each of the cards onto his score sheet in the Target column.
- Either the game may be discontinued at this point, or the same procedure may be followed on successive days until a total of 100 trials has been achieved.

Out of 100 trials, the average score to be expected from pure chance alone is 50 percent, or 50 hits per run of 100 calls. Correct guesses of 60 or more could be considered significant and beyond chance.

Precognition Test 2

Guess What Order the Cards Will Be in Tomorrow (for Older Children)

EQUIPMENT NEEDED
- Ordinary deck of playing cards
- Pencils and score sheets

INSTRUCTIONS
- The day before the test is to be conducted, the tester asks the children to write down 25 of the playing cards in the order they think the cards will come out when they are drawn from the deck of cards on the following day.
- The children are to indicate both the number and the suit of each card, writing their responses on the score sheet in the appropriate column. Score sheets are then given to the tester until the next day.
- On the day after the responses have been written, the tester shuffles the deck of cards, and turns over the first 25 one by one. (It is enjoyable for the children to participate, each taking a turn in flipping over the cards.) The tester then enters each of the cards onto his score sheet in the Target column.
- Either the game may be discontinued at this point, or the same procedure may be followed on successive days until a total of 100 trials has been achieved.

In scoring this test, 2 points will be allowed for a "full hit" (that is, guessing both the suit and the number of the card), 1 point for a numerical hit, and ½ point for a suit hit. In other words: Guessing the suit is 1 out of 4 chances (25 out of 100 is pure chance). Guessing the number is 1 out of 13 chances (8 out of 100 is pure chance). Guessing both number and suit is 1 out of 52 chances (2 out of 100 is chance).

In the total of 100 trials (with the above scoring), a score of 29 or more could be considered significant. The higher the tally, the stronger the indication of precognitive ability.

Psychometry Test 1

Touch the Red or Black Card

SPECIAL NOTE

It is suggested that this test be conducted with one child at a time and is probably most readily done at home.

EQUIPMENT NEEDED

- Ordinary deck of playing cards
- Pencil and score sheet

INSTRUCTIONS

- The tester explains the nature of the test: The child is to touch the sides of the cards, without looking at them, and when he "feels" that a card is red or black, he announces the color of the card and "cuts" the cards clean at that moment.
- The tester retains the score sheet throughout the test, and the color announced by the child is entered in the response

column by the tester. Both the tester and the child are permitted to see the exposed target card, which is then entered in the Target column.

- The cards are reshuffled after every 5 trials, approximately, so that no cutting pattern is established. The test is resumed and continued in the same manner as above for 25 calls.
- Depending on the attention span of the child, the test may be continued at this point, or on successive days, until a total of 100 tries is achieved.

SCORING AND EVALUATION

Fifty correct guesses out of 100 is pure chance. Sixty or more accurate guesses is considered significant.

Psychometry Test 2

Touch the Jack

SPECIAL NOTE

It is suggested that this test be conducted with one child at a time and is probably best done at home.

EQUIPMENT NEEDED

- Ordinary deck of playing cards
- Pencil and score sheet

INSTRUCTIONS

- The tester tells the children they are to "cut" the deck and find a jack. By feeling the cards on the side, at the moment the child "feels" he has located the jack, the child cuts clean, exposing a card.

- The tester shuffles the deck and hands the cards, facedown, to the child.
- The child tells his mind to cut a jack. By feeling the cards, when he feels he has located jack, the child cuts the cards, showing the card.
- As the tester reshuffles the deck, the child enters his response on the score sheet. Afterward, the tester enters it on his score sheet. The cards are once more handed to child to "feel" the jack in the deck of cards and to cut the deck at that point.
- The test continues until the 25 call runs are completed. The test may then be stopped and continued on another day, or continued until 100 trials have been made.

SCORING AND EVALUATION

Chance is 2 out of 100 trials. Four or more correct guesses out of 100 would be considered significant.

Dowsing Test 1

The Alphabet Dowsing Test

SPECIAL NOTE

It is suggested that this test be conducted at home. It will be helpful in this test if an assistant to the tester can score the child's response while the child is maneuvering the dowsing pendulum. If this is not possible, the child can enter the response himself.

EQUIPMENT NEEDED
- Sheets of paper

- Dowsing pendulum (which can be constructed out of a piece of string and a small metal object or button)

- The tester sketches 26 large blocks containing the 26 letters of the alphabet on two pieces of paper (a carbon copy can be made).
- The tester gives one sheet of the alphabet blocks to the child and retains one for himself.
- In another area of the room, away from the child's view (or in a nearby room) the tester places a penny or any small object over one of the letters.
- The tester announces "Target," upon which the child "tells" the dowsing pendulum to go into a circular movement and to stop when it reaches the target letter. The child holds the dowsing pendulum over the letters, going down the line from A to Z, moving along slowly until the pendulum starts to move in a circular motion. When the circular movement occurs or stops over a letter, that letter is the response call.
- Approximately 25 to 30 seconds' response time is allotted, after which the response is entered on the child's score sheet. If there is no response on one try, it should be left blank on the score sheet and considered a miss. The test should be resumed as above.
- The tester enters the target object on his score sheet and covers another letter. (The target should be selected on a random basis and not in alphabetical order.) The test continues in the same manner as above until 25 targets have been called, at which point the test is discontinued for this day. On successive days, the test is continued, depending upon the interest and attention span of the child, until a total of 100 trials have been made.

One correct guess in 25 would be chance. Out of 100 tries, four would be chance and six or more would be considered significant.

Dowsing Test 2

The Map Test

SPECIAL NOTE

It is suggested that this test be conducted at home. It will be helpful in this test if an assistant to the tester can enter the child's response while the child is maneuvering with the dowsing pendulum. If this is not possible, the child can enter the response himself.

EQUIPMENT NEEDED

- Sheets of paper
- Dowsing pendulum (which can be constructed out of a piece of string and a small metal object or button)

INSTRUCTIONS

- The tester sketches out on two sheets of paper (a carbon copy can be made) a map of the United States and prints in the names of the 50 states.
- The tester gives one sheet of the drawn map to the child and retains one copy.
- In another area of the room or in a nearby room (away from the child's view) the tester randomly places a penny or any small object over one of the states on his map.
- The tester announces "Target," and child "tells" the dowsing

pendulum to go into a circular movement and to stop when it reaches the target designated by the tester.

- The child holds the dowsing pendulum over the map, moving along slowly until the pendulum starts to move in a circular motion. When the circular movement occurs or stops over a state on the map, that is the response call. If there is no response on one try, it should be left blank on the score sheet and considered a miss, and the test should be resumed as above.

- Approximately 25 to 30 seconds' response time is allotted. The tester enters the target object on his score sheet, at random, selects the next target, and places the penny on it. The test continues in the same manner until 25 targets have been called, at which point the test is discontinued for the day. On successive days, the test is continued, depending upon the interest and attention span of the child, until a total of 100 trials have been made.

SCORING AND EVALUATION

One out of 50 correct guesses is pure chance, as is 2 out of 100. Four or more correct guesses out of 100 would be considered significant.

Score Sheets and Illustrations

STANDARD ESP SCORE SHEET*

NAME OF CHILD _____   TYPE OF TEST _____

DATE _____   NUMBER OF CORRECT HITS _____

HITS BY CHANCE ALONE _____

Column 1		Column 2		Column 3		Column 4	
TARGET	RESPONSE	TARGET	RESPONSE	TARGET	RESPONSE	TARGET	RESPONSE
1		1		1		1	
2		2		2		2	
3		3		3		3	
4		4		4		4	
5		5		5		5	
6		6		6		6	
7		7		7		7	
8		8		8		8	
9		9		9		9	
10		10		10		10	
11		11		11		11	
12		12		12		12	
13		13		13		13	
14		14		14		14	
15		15		15		15	
16		16		16		16	
17		17		17		17	
18		18		18		18	
19		19		19		19	
20		20		20		20	
21		21		21		21	
22		22		22		22	
23		23		23		23	
24		24		24		24	
25		25		25		25	

HITS _____   HITS _____   HITS _____   HITS _____

FIVE-OBJECT ESP SCORE SHEET*

NAME OF CHILD _____ TYPE OF TEST _____

DATE _____ NUMBER OF CORRECT HITS _____

HITS BY CHANCE ALONE _____

APPLE	BANANAS	CAR	DUCK	ELEPHANT

| A | B | C | D | E |

| TARGET | RESPONSE | | TARGET | RESPONSE | | TARGET | RESPONSE | | TARGET | RESPONSE |

1 2 3 4 5 6 7 8 9 10 11 12 13 14 15 16 17 18 19 20 21 22 23 24 25

HITS _____   HITS _____   HITS _____   HITS _____

* The Five-Object Score Sheet incorporates an optional step in which the five target objects have been sketched in miniature to assist the children in spontaneous responses.

Following are five objects that may be used as symbols in testing. Testers may copy or trace them for tests in the classroom or at home. You may wish to improvise and use symbols or other designs.

Figure 4

APPLE

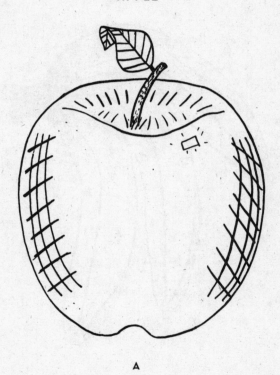

A

Figure 5

BANANAS

B

Figure 6

CAR

C

Figure 7

DUCK

D

Figure 8

ELEPHANT

E

DEVISE YOUR OWN TEST SCORE SHEET*

NAME OF CHILD _____   TYPE OF TEST _____

DATE _____   NUMBER OF CORRECT HITS _____

HITS BY CHANCE ALONE _____

Column 1	Column 2	Column 3	Column 4

	TARGET	RESPONSE		TARGET	RESPONSE		TARGET	RESPONSE		TARGET	RESPONSE
1			1			1			1		
2			2			2			2		
3			3			3			3		
4			4			4			4		
5			5			5			5		
6			6			6			6		
7			7			7			7		
8			8			8			8		
9			9			9			9		
10			10			10			10		
11			11			11			11		
12			12			12			12		
13			13			13			13		
14			14			14			14		
15			15			15			15		
16			16			16			16		
17			17			17			17		
18			18			18			18		
19			19			19			19		
20			20			20			20		
21			21			21			21		
22			22			22			22		
23			23			23			23		
24			24			24			24		
25			25			25			25		

HITS _____   HITS _____   HITS _____   HITS _____

* You may want to try your hand at devising a new test. The above score sheet may be utilized should you wish to improvise.

Thirteen

Summing Up

Ours is an ever-expanding universe. Changes are being made at a pace that was unknown to our grandparents. What is in its infancy today may be full-blown in twenty-five years and "old hat" in fifty. This is particularly true in the field of parapsychology. Although the testing of children to develop their psi abilities is relatively new, fifty years from now what we are doing today will indeed be "child's play." In future generations, children, using their psychic abilities, may lead us into an expanded consciousness and a better understanding of the true nature of man.

If children are to utilize their psychic awareness in everyday endeavors, it must be activated by their parents and teachers by the faith they place in their children, by the understanding shown them. Once adults realize that children have psychic experiences, they must help them open up by opening up first, by listening to what they are saying. Parents and teachers alike should try to foster children's CPE—Creative Perceptive Energy—by accepting it as a natural gift that can be enhanced through the ESP testing program outlined in this book.

As a child develops, certain psychic components may be very noticeable, while others may remain dormant. These hidden abilities can come to the fore in later years. True psychic abilities, whatever the category, are never lost; they always find a variety of ways to manifest themselves.

It is left to adults to explain to children that they are not to be afraid of their psychic experiences. Their psychic ability may well be compared to electricity. We know it exists, we know how to apply it, but we do not know its essence. We can't hold it or touch it, but we do know how to use it. It has always existed, but we have "discovered" it. It is the same with any psychic phenomenon. We do not know the essence of it, but we are beginning to learn how to apply it.

Athena Drewes tells us that children are a lot more open about ESP than adults but that ESP in children is prone to go underground unless the environment at home stimulates the development of their psychic abilities.

In "A Two-Year Program of Tests for Clairvoyance and Precognition with a Class of Public School Pupils," an article in the September 1959 issue of the *Journal of Parapsychology*, Margaret Anderson and Elsie Gregory describe the excellent results that can be obtained with a group of children in classroom ESP tests over a two-year period. It also bore out our theories that the amount of interest and success displayed by the students was in direct relation to the enthusiasm and understanding of the adult involved—in this case the teacher, but in other instances the parents acting as testers.

A professional student of parapsychology told us an interesting story. She had a five-year-old daughter who was rather withdrawn and "always seemed to be moping around the house." One day, the student and her sister were sitting in the kitchen having afternoon tea. The student had not seen her sister for several months, so they were catching up on recent events. Her sister told her about a series of strange dreams she was having that were frightening her: "I see myself floating above my body. Then I drift out into the garden and go down the road to the lake. Suddenly I come back in a flash and return to my sleeping body." The student laughed and told her sister not to be upset, that what she was having were out-of-body experiences. At that point, the student's young daughter, who was listening intently, blurted out that she was having these same types of dreams but had been afraid of telling her mother or father. The young girl said she was scared her father would punish her for making up stories. The mother told her daughter that she should never be afraid to tell either of her parents about any so-called strange experiences and reassured her that they were natural happenings that most people experienced at one time or another.

The student went on to relate that at an earlier point in her marriage her husband had been somewhat skeptical of her interest in ESP and that it was only over a period of time that he stopped ridiculing her activities in this area. He told his wife that he realized that no experience should be looked down upon, whether you believed in it or not. They had discussed the effect skeptics might have on those who experience ESP and concluded that no human being ever wants to be ridiculed. Apparently, their child had picked up some of the telepathic waves here and had been too frightened to speak of her experiences. Once this came out, and she realized she would not be rebuked by either of her parents, the child changed her attitude considerably. Where she had previously thrown up roadblocks when it came to going to school, she now looked forward to playing with her classmates. Where she had been silent and withdrawn, she suddenly was radiant with animated conversation. "She grew to trust us and was no longer frightened." Thus we see how a parent's understanding and natural treatment turned a potentially dangerous situation into a positive one.

Today events move quickly. It seems as though it was only yesterday that we were watching silent films, before the creative innovators of the motion-picture industry began to follow the signs that would lead to today's talkies, with voices, color, and music. Wasn't it only yesterday that Franklin Delano Roosevelt was stricken with polio, triggering a nationwide drive by the March of Dimes to combat that menace? Through man's creativity, the Salk vaccine has greatly reduced the incidence of polio in the world today.

It was also only yesterday that we were held so captive by superstition, scorn, ignorance, and fear that we were unable to ask questions about psychic matters. But today is a new day, and we approach a new era. Perhaps Ambrose A. Worrall, author of *Explore Your Psychic World* and a man beloved by all in the psychic field, sums it up best:

> It's a new day, in which we are at last able to explore questions without having to face the mockery of science, the church's fear of demonic invasion, or the cynicism and skepticism of a public that has waited long for facts it could rely on. It is the harbinger of a new era in which the truth all of us carry within ourselves can be brought at last into the sunlight of outer day and the timeless yearnings of all of us for truth.[1]

Together let us—medical authorities, psychiatrists, psychologists, parapsychologists, parents, teachers, adults, children—follow the signs to emerging breakthroughs in new dimensions. For the truths that we dare to seek and the horizons that we dare to explore may well determine our destiny as human beings.

In the beginning God created the Heaven and the earth. And the earth was without form, and void; and darkness was upon the face of the deep. And the Spirit of God moved upon the face of the waters. And God said, Let there be light; and there was light [Genesis 1:1-3].

Acknowledgments

The authors wish to express their deep gratitude to:

Robert Levine, our brilliant and very special editor, who understood what it was we wanted to say and helped us to say it.

John H. Donnelly, wise in so many ways, whose guiding hand and heart were given many times into the wee hours in order that we might accomplish this work.

Rose Fair, for her steadfast faith and encouragement.

Jane Herman, whose fine hand, guidance, and checking of last-minute details added immeasurably to the appearance and content of this book.

Ruth and James Hannon, without whose help and support this book could not have been completed.

Berthold Schwarz, who bolstered and encouraged us from the beginning and provided us with keen insight and much helpful material to aid parents and children in understanding.

Vera Webster, for her penetrating foresight into matters that concern children.

Athena A. Drewes, a brick from the onset who readily gave of her time and energy to read the manuscript and discuss test methods, and who never failed to respond with warm enthusiasm.

Eloise Shields, who sent us marvelous anecdotes and personal experiences with detailed information concerning children in the classroom and out of it, and who also kindly read our manuscript.

Harold Sherman, that wise pioneer of ESP, for his wonderful support and help in countless ways.

Rhea A. White, for her eagle eye and excellent guidance in suggested readings and preparation of the bibliography.

Amy Sue Arkind, for the splendid illustrations in the test section of the book.

Anne Lunt, for her many helpful suggestions to the manuscript.

This book would not be complete without grateful acknowledgment to William Griffin and Toni Lopopolo for their many kindnesses and courtesies.

And the many other individuals who provided help: Marc C. Arkind, Mary Ellen Casey, the Fair family, Betty J. Kelly, Andrea Fodor Litkei, Marian Nester, Joan Paris, Leslie Price, John L. Travis, Olga Worrall, Ruby Yeatman, and the Zomper family.

Very special thanks are given to the students, teachers, and parents who permitted us to draw from their experiences, some of whom have not been identified by their real names in order to protect confidentiality.

Notes

INTRODUCTION

1. Harold Sherman. *How to Make ESP Work for You* (New York: Fawcett Crest, CBS Publications; first published by DeVorss, 1964).
2. Ibid.
3. Ibid.
4. Ibid.

1. KNOWING WHAT IS PSYCHIC

1. Katherine Fair Donnelly. *The Guidebook to ESP and Psychic Wonders* (New York: David McKay, 1978).

3. IMAGINARY PLAYMATES

1. Ambrose A. and Olga N. Worrall, with W. Oursler. *Explore Your Psychic World* (New York: Harper & Row, 1970).
2. Berthold E. Schwarz. "Family Telepathy," *Psychic* 3, 5 (March/April 1972).

4. PSYCHIC DREAMS

1. Carl G. Jung. *Civilization in Transition*, vol. 10 of *The Collected Works of C. G. Jung*, trans. R. F. C. Hull (Princeton, NJ, and New York: Princeton University Press, Bollingen Series, 1964).

6. THE CHILD FROM CONCEPTION TO THE SIXTH YEAR

1. Jan Ehrenwald. "Mother-Child Symbiosis: Cradle of ESP," *Psychoanalytic Review* 58, 3 (1971).
2. Ibid.

7. EDUCATING THE TWO SIDES OF THE BRAIN

1. J.E. Bogen. "Education and Hemisphere Process of the Brain," *UCLA Educator* 17, 2 (Spring 1975).
2. Paul F. Brandwein. *The Reduction of Complexity* (New York: International Center for Educational Advancement, Harcourt Brace Jovanovich, 1977).
3. Paul F. Brandwein and Robert Ornstein. "The Duality of the Mind," *Instructor* (January 1977).
4. Michael S. Gazzaniga. "Review of the Split Brain," UCLA Foundation, Graduate School of Education, *UCLA Educator* 17, 2 (Spring 1975).

8. PSYCHIC DEVELOPMENT OF THE CHILD

1. Boston Society for Psychic Research, Boston, 1928. (Reprinted New Hyde Park, NY: University Books, 1963.)
2. Gardner Murphy. "Creativity and Its Relationship to Extrasensory Perception," *Journal of the American Society for Psychical Research* (October 1963): 204.
3. Gardner Murphy. "The Discovery of Gifted Sensitives," *Journal of the American Society for Psychical Research* (January 1969): 16.
4. John Sanbonmatsu. "Letter from a Reader," *American Society of Psychical Research Newsletter* 3, 3 (July 1977).
5. Upton Sinclair. *Mental Radio* (Springfield, IL: Charles C. Thomas, 1962). Originally published by Werner Laurie, 1930.
6. R. A. McConnell. *ESP Curriculum Guide* (New York: Simon & Schuster, 1970).

9. TEST INFORMATION AND INSTRUCTIONS FOR PARENTS AND TEACHERS

1. Louisa E. Rhine. *PSI: What Is It?* (New York: Harper & Row, 1975).
2. Athena A. Drewes and Sally A. Drucker. "Children and ESP," *American Society of Psychical Research Newsletter* 3, 3 (July 1977):
3. Louisa E. Rhine. *PSI: What Is It?*

13. SUMMING UP

1. Ambrose A. and Olga N. Worrall, with W. Oursler. *Explore Your Psychic World* (New York: Harper & Row, 1970).

Glossary

AGENT: The person transmitting a telepathic message or thought.

ASTRAL PROJECTION: The act of some part of the self—the soul or the spirit—leaving the physical body temporarily, which can occur while a person is awake or asleep. According to this theory, the mind can wander freely and return to the body at will. See *Out-of-body experience*.

AURA: The halo or light that surrounds every human being. The aura has been called an emanation of the human spirit.

BILOCATION: The state of being physically in two places at the same time.

CALL: The symbol selected by the subject of an ESP test when he or she attempts to guess a target. See *Response*.

CHANCE: The possibility of something happening by pure luck. Chance occurrence is what can be expected in simple guesswork.

CLAIRVOYANCE: The perception of distant events or people without the use of the physical senses. Being able to "see" a distant event while it is occurring.

CPE:	Creative Perceptive Energy
DAYDREAM:	A reverie consisting of one or more pleasing visions or anticipations that may be in the realm of the possible.
DISCARNATE:	The spirit or intelligence of a human or animal that lives on after death.
DOWN THROUGH:	A way to test for clairvoyance in which cards are called down through a deck before they are cut and checked.
DOWSING:	The use of an inanimate object, such as a stick or branch or string with a small metal item attached, to detect lost objects or to discover water, oil, or metals underground.
ESP:	ExtraSensory Perception—the state of being aware of thoughts, objects, or events without the use of the normal physical senses.
FANTASY:	The product of a person's imagination, especially an illusory image or thought that cannot come true.
HALLUCINATION:	"Seeing" objects that are not real. Also experiencing sensations that have no external cause. Any extreme form of delusion.
HIT:	A correct answer in an ESP test. See *Target*.
MEDITATION:	Deep and continued thought on some particular subject or pleasant experience with a view to relaxation.
OUT-OF-BODY EXPERIENCE:	The traveling of some part of the self, such as the spirit or soul, through space or time. The physical body is left behind either at rest or asleep. See *Astral projection*.

PARANORMAL:	Beyond or above normal means.
PARAPSYCHOLOGY:	The name given to the study of psi (psychic) events, such as clairvoyance, telepathy, precognition, etc.
PERCIPIENT:	The person who receives telepathic or clairvoyant impressions in an ESP test situation.
PLACEMENT PK TEST:	A test in which a subject attempts to move objects from one place to another without exerting any physical force.
PRECOGNITION:	The knowledge of an event that has not happened yet when there is no possibility of advance knowledge.
PSI:	A general term used to denote psychical phenomena. Also called ESP.
PSYCHOKINESIS (PK):	The influence a person exerts upon an object without the use of known physical force. The moving of an object by use of mental power.
RANDOM SERIES:	A series of numbers or figures in which each member is independent of the others.
RETROCOGNITION:	"Seeing" past events without any knowledge of them. Knowledge of the past without the use of the normal five senses.
RESPONSE:	The answer given by a subject in an ESP test. It is supposed to represent the target being "sent" by the agent. Similar to *Call*.
RUN (OR CALL RUN):	The series of trials in an ESP test.
SUBJECT:	A person who is the receiver in an ESP test.
TARGET:	The symbol or object used in an ESP test, generally "sent" by an agent.

TELEPATHY: The receiving or sending of thought messages of any kind from one person to another. The awareness of someone's thoughts at the moment he or she is thinking them.

TRIAL: Each single call of a receiver in an ESP test with cards or objects.

Bibliography

Anderson, M. L., and R. A. White "A Survey of Work on ESP and Teacher-Pupil Attitudes," *Journal of Parapsychology* 22 (1958):246–68.

Beadle, Muriel. *A Child's Mind.* Garden City, NY: Doubleday, 1970.

Birren, Faber. *Color: A Survey in Words and Pictures.* New Hyde Park, NY: University Books, 1963.

Bogen, J. E. "Education and Hemisphere Process of the Brain," *UCLA Educator* 17, 2 (Spring 1975):

Bond, Esther May. "General Extra-sensory Perception with a Group of Fourth and Fifth Grade Retarded Children," *Journal of Parapsychology* 1 (1937):114–22.

Brandwein, Paul F. *The Reduction of Complexity.* New York: Harcourt Brace Jovanovich, 1977.

Brier, Robert M. "A Mass School Test of Precognition," *Journal of Parapsychology* 33 (1969):125–35.

Cooke, Aileen H. *Out of the Mouths of Babes.* Cambridge and London: James Clarke, 1968.

Dean, Douglas, and John Mihalesky. *Executive ESP.* Englewood Cliffs, NJ: Prentice-Hall, 1978.

Donnelly, K. F. *The Guidebook to ESP and Psychic Wonders.* New York: David McKay, 1978.

Drewes, A. A., and S. A. Drucker. "Children and ESP," *ASPR Newsletter* 3, 3 (July 1977).

Duplessis, Yvonne. *The Paranormal Perception of Color.* New York: Parapsychology Foundation, 1975.

Ehrenwald, Jan. "Mother-Child Symbiosis: Cradle of ESP," *Psychoanalytic Review* 58, 3 (1971).

———. "Psi Phenomena in Search of a Neural Foothold," *ASPR Newsletter* 2, 3 (1976).

Fodor, Nandor. *The Search for the Beloved.* New York: Hermitage Press, 1949.

Garrett, Eileen J. *Adventures in the Supernormal.* New York: Garrett Publications, 1949.

Gazzaniga, M. S. "Review of the Split Brain." UCLA Foundation, Graduate School of Education: From *UCLA Educator* 17, 2 (Spring 1975).

Green, Celia. *Out-of-the-Body Experiences.* Oxford: Institute of Psychophysical Research, 1968.

Greenhouse, Herbert B. *The Astral Journey.* Garden City, NY: Doubleday, 1975.

Hardy, Alister, Robert Harvie, and Arthur Koestler. *The Challenge of Chance.* New York: Random House, 1974.

Heywood, Rosalind. *Beyond the Reach of Sense.* New York: E. P. Dutton, 1974.

Hintze, N. A., and J. G. Pratt. *The Psychic Realm: What Can You Believe?* New York: Random House, 1975.

LeShan, Lawrence. *How to Meditate.* Boston: Little, Brown, 1974.

———. *The Medium, the Mystic, and the Physicist.* New York: Viking, 1966.

———. *Toward a General Theory of the Paranormal.* New York: Parapsychology Foundation, 1969.

Louwerens, N. G. "ESP Experiments with Nursery School Children in the Netherlands," *Journal of Parapsychology* 24 (1960):75–93.

McConnell, R. A. *ESP: A Curriculum Guide.* New York: Simon & Schuster, 1971.

———. "ESP and Credibility in Science," *The American Psychologist* 24 (1969):531–38.

McMahan, Elizabeth. "A Review of the Evidence of Dowsing." *Journal of Parapsychology* 11 (1947):175–90.

Murphy, Gardner. "Creativity and Its Relation to Extrasensory Perception," *Journal of the American Society for Psychical Research* 57, 4 (1963).

———. "The Discovery of Gifted Sensitives," *Journal of the American Society for Psychical Research* 63, 1 (1969).

Ornstein, R. E. *The Psychology of Consciousness.* New York: Viking, 1972.

———, ed. *The Nature of Human Consciousness.* New York: Viking, 1974.

———, and Paul F. Brandwein. *The Duality of the Mind.* Dansville, NY: Instructor Publications, 1977.

Ott, John N. *Health and Light.* Old Greenwich, CT: Devin-Adair, 1973.

Palmer, John, and Carol Vassar. "ESP and Out-of-the-Body Experiences: An Exploratory Study, *Journal of the American Society for Psychical Research* 68 (1974):257–80.

Rhine, Louisa A. *ESP in Life and Lab.* New York: Macmillan, 1967.

———. *PSI: What Is It?* New York: Harper & Row, 1975.

Rogo, D. Scott. *Parapsychology: A Century of Inquiry.* New York: Dell, 1975.

Samples, Bob. *The Metaphoric Mind.* Reading, MA: Addison-Wesley, 1976.

Schwarz, Berthold E. "Clinical Studies on Telesomatic Reactions," *Medical Times* 101, 2, 71 (December 1973).

———. "Family Telepathy," *Psychic* 3, 5 (March/April 1972).

———. *Parent-Child Telepathy.* New York: Garrett Publications, 1971.

Sherman, Harold. *How to Make ESP Work for You.* New York: Fawcett, CBS Publications. First published by DeVorss, 1964.

———. "Reading Achievement as Related to ESP," *Psychic International Quarterly* 1, 1 (May 1964).

———, and Clarissa Mulders. "Pleasant Versus Unpleasant Targets on Children's ESP Tests and Their Relationship to Personality Tests," *Journal of Parapsychology* 39, 2 (June 1975):165–75.

Sinclair, Upton. *Mental Radio.* Springfield, IL: Charles C. Thomas, 1962.

Singer, Jerome L. *The Inner World of Daydreaming.* New York: Harper & Row, 1975.

Staff, Vera S. *Remembered on Waking.* Sussex, England: Churches Fellowship for Psychical and Spiritual Studies, 1975.

Tanous, Alex, with Ardman, H. *Beyond Coincidence.* Garden City, New York: Doubleday, 1976.

Tart, Charles T. "A Psychological Study of Out-of-the-Body Experiences in a Selected Subject," *Journal of the American Society for Psychical Research* 62, 3 (1968).

———. *PSI: Scientific Studies of the Psychic Realm.* New York: E. P. Dutton, 1977.

Van Busschbach, J. G. "An Investigation of ESP in the First and Second Grades of Dutch Schools," *Journal of Parapsychology* 23 (1959):227–37.

———. "An Investigation of Extrasensory Perception in School Children," *Journal of Parapsychology* 17 (1953):210–14.

Vasse, Christiane and Paul. "ESP Tests with French First-Grade School Children." *Journal of Parapsychology* 22 (1958):187–203.

Worrall, Ambrose A. and Olga N., with Will Oursler. *Explore Your Psychic World.* New York: Harper & Row, 1970.

Young, S. H. *Psychic Children.* Garden City, NY: Doubleday, 1977.

Suggested Reading

Andreae, Christine. *Seances and Spiritualists*. Philadelphia: Lippincott, 1974.

Donnelly, Katherine Fair. *The Guidebook to ESP and Psychic Wonders*. New York: David McKay, 1978.

Feola, Jose. *PK: Mind Over Matter*. Minneapolis: Dillon Press, 1975.

Heaps, Willard. *Psychic Phenomena*. Nashville: Thomas Nelson, 1974.

Knight, David. *Poltergeists: Hauntings and the Haunted*. Philadelphia: J. B. Lippincott, 1972.

McHargue, Georgess. *Facts, Frauds and Phantasms*. Garden City, NY: Doubleday, 1972.

Rhine, Louisa. *Mind Over Matter*. New York: Macmillan, 1970.

———. *PSI: What Is It?* New York: Macmillan, 1976.

Rose, Karen. *In the Land of the Mind*. New York: Atheneum, 1975.

Sherman, Harold. *How to Make ESP Work for You*. New York: Fawcett, 1974.

———. *How to Picture What You Want*. New York: Fawcett, 1978.

Tanous, Alex, with Ardman, Harvey. *Beyond Coincidence*. New York: Doubleday, 1976.

Index

Permissions